KRAFT
PHILADELPHIA
Favorite Recipes

Publications International, Ltd.

Louis Weber, CEO
Publications International, Ltd.
7373 North Cicero Avenue
Lincolnwood, IL 60712

DIGIORNO® is a registered trademark of Nestle, used under license.

TACO BELL® and HOME ORIGINALS® are trademarks owned and licensed by Taco Bell Corp.

Pictured on the front cover: Chocolate Silk Pie with Marshmallow Meringue *(page 102).*
Pictured on the back cover (clockwise from top): Barbecue Bacon Party Spread *(page 154),* Deep Dish Chicken Pot Pie *(page 208),*and Strawberry Cheesecake Squares *(page 78).*

ISBN-13: 978-1-4508-1706-6

ISBN-10: 1-4508-1706-8

Library of Congress Control Number: 2011921868

Manufactured in China.

8 7 6 5 4 3 2 1

Microwave Cooking: Microwave ovens vary in wattage. Use the cooking times as guidelines and check for doneness before adding more time.

Preparation/Cooking Times: Preparation times are based on the approximate amount of time required to assemble the recipe before cooking, baking, chilling or serving. These times include preparation steps such as measuring, chopping and mixing. The fact that some preparations and cooking can be done simultaneously is taken into account. Preparation of optional ingredients and serving suggestions is not included.

Table of Contents

PHILADELPHIA

KRAFT

Tips for the Perfect Cheesecake

For best quality and results, always use **PHILADELPHIA** Cream Cheese.

PREHEATING THE OVEN: The baking time indicated in a recipe is based on using a preheated oven. Turn the oven on when you start to mix the cheesecake ingredients. This should allow enough time for the oven to heat to the correct temperature for when you are ready to place the cheesecake in the oven for baking. Unless otherwise indicated, always bake cheesecakes in the center of the middle oven rack.

BEATING THE BATTER: While adding ingredients, do not overbeat the cheesecake batter. Too much air beaten into the batter will result in a cheesecake that sinks in the center when cooled.

BAKING CHEESECAKES: Overbaked cheesecakes will tend to crack. Remove cheesecake from oven when center is almost set (i.e., center of cheesecake still wiggles when pan is gently shaken from side-to-side). Although the cheesecake appears underbaked, the residual heat in the cheesecake will be enough to finish baking the center. After chilling, the cheesecake will have a perfectly smooth consistency.

COOLING CHEESECAKES: Cool cheesecakes completely before refrigerating. Placing a still-warm cheesecake in the refrigerator will cause condensation to form on the cake, resulting in a soggy cheesecake.

CUTTING CHEESECAKES: Cut cheesecakes when they are cold rather than warm. Use a sharp knife with a clean thin blade. To make clean cuts, dip the knife in hot water after each cut and wipe the blade clean.

For all of your occasions, **PHILLY MAKES A BETTER CHEESECAKE.**

During tests of plain New York style cheesecake made with **PHILADELPHIA** Cream Cheese versus store-branded cream cheese, consumers rated **PHILLY** cheesecake as better tasting.

Fruity Favorites

PHILADELPHIA Peaches 'n Cream No-Bake Cheesecake

Prep: 15 min. plus refrigerating

2 cups **HONEY MAID** Graham Cracker Crumbs

6 Tbsp. margarine, melted

1 cup sugar, divided

4 pkg. (8 oz. each) **PHILADELPHIA** Neufchâtel Cheese, softened

1 pkg. (4-serving size) **JELL-O** Peach Flavor Gelatin

2 fresh peaches, chopped

1 tub (8 oz.) **COOL WHIP LITE** Whipped Topping, thawed

MIX graham crumbs, margarine and ¼ cup of the sugar; press firmly onto bottom of 13×9-inch pan. Refrigerate while preparing filling.

BEAT Neufchâtel cheese and remaining ¾ cup sugar in large bowl with electric mixer on medium speed until well blended. Add dry gelatin mix; mix until blended. Stir in peaches. Gently stir in whipped topping. Spoon over crust; cover.

REFRIGERATE 4 hours or until firm. Store leftovers in refrigerator.

Makes 16 servings, 1 piece each.

SUBSTITUTE: Prepare as directed using 1 drained 15-oz. can peaches.

White Chocolate-Cranberry Cheesecake

Prep: 15 min. • Bake: 50 min.

1¼ cups **OREO** Chocolate Cookie Crumbs

¼ cup butter, melted

3 pkg. (8 oz. each) **PHILADELPHIA** Cream Cheese, softened

¾ cup sugar

3 eggs

4 squares **BAKER'S** White Chocolate, melted

½ cup dried cranberries

1 tsp. grated orange peel

PREHEAT oven to 350°F. Mix cookie crumbs and butter. Press firmly onto bottom of 9-inch springform pan.

BEAT cream cheese and sugar in large bowl with electric mixer on medium speed until well blended. Add eggs, 1 at a time, mixing just until blended after each addition. Stir in white chocolate, cranberries and orange peel; pour over crust.

BAKE 45 to 50 min. or until center is almost set if using a silver springform pan. (Or, bake at 325°F for 45 to 50 min. if using a dark nonstick springform pan.) Cool completely. Refrigerate 3 hours or overnight.

Makes 12 servings.

JAZZ IT UP: Garnish with thawed COOL WHIP Whipped Topping, orange slices, and additional dried cranberries.

PHILADELPHIA Strawberry Fields
No-Bake Cheesecake

Prep: 15 min. plus refrigerating

- 2 cups **HONEY MAID** Graham Cracker Crumbs
- 6 Tbsp. margarine, melted
- 1 cup sugar, divided
- 4 pkg. (8 oz. each) **PHILADELPHIA** Neufchâtel Cheese, softened
- ½ cup strawberry preserves
- 1 pkg. (16 oz.) frozen strawberries, thawed, drained
- 1 tub (8 oz.) **COOL WHIP LITE** Whipped Topping, thawed

MIX graham crumbs, margarine and ¼ cup of the sugar; press firmly onto bottom of 13×9-inch pan. Refrigerate while preparing filling.

BEAT Neufchâtel cheese and remaining ¾ cup sugar in large bowl with electric mixer on medium speed until well blended. Add preserves; mix until blended. Stir in strawberries. Gently stir in whipped topping. Spoon over crust; cover.

REFRIGERATE 4 hours or until firm. Store leftovers in refrigerator.

Makes 16 servings, 1 piece each.

HOW TO MAKE IT WITH FRESH STRAWBERRIES: Place 2 cups fresh strawberries in small bowl with additional 2 Tbsp. sugar; mash with fork. Add to Neufchâtel cheese mixture; continue as directed.

White Chocolate Cherry Pecan Cheesecake

Prep: 30 min. • Bake: 1 hour

1 cup **PLANTERS** Pecan Halves, toasted, divided

1½ cups **HONEY MAID** Graham Cracker Crumbs

¼ cup sugar

¼ cup margarine or butter, melted

3 pkg. (8 oz. each) **PHILADELPHIA** Cream Cheese, softened

1 can (14 oz.) sweetened condensed milk

1 pkg. (6 squares) **BAKER'S** White Chocolate, melted

2 tsp. vanilla, divided

4 eggs

1 can (21 oz.) cherry pie filling

1 cup thawed **COOL WHIP** Whipped Topping

PREHEAT oven to 300°F if using a silver 9-inch springform pan (or to 275°F if using a dark nonstick 9-inch springform pan). Reserve 16 of the pecan halves for garnish. Finely chop remaining pecans; mix with graham crumbs, sugar and margarine. Press firmly onto bottom of pan.

BEAT cream cheese in large bowl with electric mixer on medium speed until creamy. Gradually add sweetened condensed milk, beating until well blended. Add chocolate and 1 tsp. of the vanilla; mix well. Add eggs, 1 at a time, mixing on low speed after each addition just until blended. Pour over crust.

BAKE 1 hour or until center is almost set. Run knife or metal spatula around rim of pan to loosen cake; cool before removing rim of pan. Refrigerate 4 hours or overnight.

MIX pie filling and remaining 1 tsp. vanilla; spoon over cheesecake. Top with whipped topping and reserved pecans. Cut into wedges to serve. Store leftover cheesecake in refrigerator.

Makes 16 servings.

Vanilla Cherry Cheesecake

Prep: 15 min. • Bake: 40 min.

2 pkg. (8 oz. each) **PHILADELPHIA Cream Cheese, softened**

⅓ cup **GENERAL FOODS INTERNATIONAL Vanilla Crème**

¼ cup sugar

¼ cup milk

2 eggs

1 **HONEY MAID Pie Crust (6 oz.)**

1 cup cherry pie filling

PREHEAT oven to 325°F. Beat cream cheese, vanilla beverage mix and sugar in large bowl with electric mixer on medium speed until well blended. Gradually add milk, beating until well blended. Add eggs, 1 at a time, beating just until blended after each addition. Pour into crust.

BAKE 40 min. or until center is almost set. Cool.

REFRIGERATE 3 hours or overnight. Top with cherry pie filling just before serving. Store leftover cheesecake in refrigerator.

Makes 10 servings.

Wave-Your-Flag Cheesecake

Prep: 20 min. plus refrigerating

1 qt. strawberries, divided

1½ cups boiling water

2 pkg. (4-serving size each) **JELL-O** Strawberry Flavor Gelatin

Ice cubes

1 cup cold water

1 pkg. (10.75 oz.) pound cake, cut into 10 slices

2 pkg. (8 oz. each) **PHILADELPHIA** Cream Cheese, softened

¼ cup sugar

1 tub (8 oz.) **COOL WHIP** Whipped Topping, thawed

1 cup blueberries

SLICE 1 cup of the strawberries; set aside. Halve the remaining 3 cups strawberries; set aside. Stir boiling water into dry gelatin mixes in large bowl at least 2 min. until completely dissolved. Add enough ice to cold water to measure 2 cups. Add to gelatin; stir until ice is completely melted. Refrigerate 5 min. or until gelatin is slightly thickened (consistency of unbeaten egg whites).

MEANWHILE, line bottom of 13×9-inch dish with cake slices. Add sliced strawberries to thickened gelatin; stir gently. Spoon over cake slices. Refrigerate 4 hours or until set.

BEAT cream cheese and sugar in large bowl with wire whisk or electric mixer until well blended; gently stir in whipped topping. Spread over gelatin. Arrange strawberry halves on cream cheese mixture to resemble the stripes of a flag. Arrange blueberries on cream cheese mixture for the stars. Store any leftover dessert in refrigerator.

Makes 20 servings.

Triple-Citrus Cheesecake

Prep: 30 min. ● Bake: 1 hour 5 min.

1 cup **HONEY MAID** Graham Cracker Crumbs

⅓ cup firmly packed brown sugar

¼ cup butter or margarine, melted

4 pkg. (8 oz. each) **PHILADELPHIA** Cream Cheese, softened

1 cup granulated sugar

2 Tbsp. flour

1 tsp. vanilla

4 eggs

1 Tbsp. fresh lemon juice

1 Tbsp. fresh lime juice

1 Tbsp. fresh orange juice

1 tsp. grated lemon peel

1 tsp. grated lime peel

1 tsp. grated orange peel

PREHEAT oven to 325°F if using a silver 9-inch springform pan (or to 300°F if using a dark nonstick 9-inch springform pan). Mix graham crumbs, brown sugar and butter; press firmly onto bottom of pan. Bake 10 min.

BEAT cream cheese, granulated sugar, flour and vanilla with electric mixer on medium speed until well blended. Add eggs, 1 at a time, mixing on low speed after each addition just until blended. Stir in remaining ingredients; pour over crust.

BAKE 1 hour and 5 min., or until center is almost set. Run knife or metal spatula around rim of pan to loosen cake; cool before removing rim of pan. Refrigerate 4 hours or overnight. Garnish as desired. Store leftover cheesecake in refrigerator.

Makes 16 servings.

Triple-Berry Cheesecake Tart

Prep: 15 min. plus refrigerating

1¼ cups finely crushed **NILLA Wafers (about 45 wafers)**

¼ cup butter, melted

1 pkg. (8 oz.) **PHILADELPHIA** Cream Cheese, softened

¼ cup sugar

1 cup thawed **COOL WHIP** Whipped Topping

2 cups mixed berries (raspberries, sliced strawberries and blueberries)

¾ cup boiling water

1 pkg. (4-serving size) **JELL-O** Lemon Flavor Gelatin

1 cup ice cubes

MIX wafer crumbs and butter in small bowl until well blended. Press onto bottom and up side of 9-inch tart pan. Place in freezer while preparing filling.

BEAT cream cheese and sugar in large bowl with electric mixer on medium speed until well blended. Gently stir in whipped topping. Spoon into crust; top with berries. Cover and refrigerate.

STIR boiling water into dry gelatin mix in medium bowl 2 min. until completely dissolved. Add ice cubes; stir until ice is completely melted. Refrigerate about 15 min. or until slightly thickened (consistency of unbeaten egg whites). Spoon gelatin over fruit in pan. Refrigerate 3 hours.

Makes 10 servings.

Lemon Cheesecake

Prep: 15 min. ● Bake: 50 min.

1½ cups **HONEY MAID** Graham Cracker Crumbs, finely crushed

1¼ cups sugar, divided

3 Tbsp. butter or margarine, melted

3 pkg. (8 oz. each) **PHILADELPHIA** Cream Cheese, softened

1 cup **BREAKSTONE'S** or **KNUDSEN** Sour Cream

Grated peel and juice from 1 medium lemon

3 eggs

PREHEAT oven to 350°F if using a silver 9-inch springform pan (or to 325°F if using a dark nonstick 9-inch springform pan). Mix graham crumbs, ¼ cup of the sugar and butter. Reserve ½ cup of the crumb mixture; press remaining crumb mixture firmly onto bottom of pan. Set aside.

BEAT cream cheese and remaining 1 cup sugar in large bowl with electric mixer on medium speed until well blended. Add sour cream, lemon peel and juice; mix well. Add eggs, 1 at a time, beating on low speed after each addition just until blended. Pour over crust; sprinkle with reserved crumb mixture.

BAKE 45 to 50 min. or until center is almost set. Turn off oven. Open door slightly; let cheesecake stand in oven 30 min. Remove to wire rack. Run knife or metal spatula around rim of pan to loosen cake; cool before removing rim of pan. Refrigerate at least 4 hours or overnight. Garnish as desired. Store leftover cheesecake in refrigerator.

Makes 12 servings.

HOW TO SOFTEN CREAM CHEESE: Place completely unwrapped packages of cream cheese on microwaveable plate. Microwave on HIGH 15 to 20 sec. or until slightly softened.

Fruity Cheesecake

Prep: 30 min. ● Bake: 1 hour

1 cup crushed **NILLA** Wafers (about 25 wafers)

3 Tbsp. butter or margarine, melted

3 Tbsp. sugar

4 pkg. (8 oz. each) **PHILADELPHIA** Cream Cheese, softened

1 cup sugar

2 Tbsp. flour

1 cup **BREAKSTONE'S** or **KNUDSEN** Sour Cream

4 eggs

1 pkg. (4-serving size) **JELL-O** Lemon Flavor Instant Pudding & Pie Filling

2 cups thawed **COOL WHIP** Whipped Topping

1 cup each: blueberries, sliced strawberries and peeled sliced kiwi

PREHEAT oven to 325°F. Line 13×9-inch baking pan with foil, with ends of foil extending over sides. Mix wafer crumbs, butter and 3 Tbsp. sugar; press firmly onto bottom of pan. Bake 10 min.

BEAT cream cheese, 1 cup sugar and the flour in large bowl with electric mixer on medium speed until well blended. Add sour cream; mix well. Add eggs, 1 at a time, mixing on low speed after each addition just until blended. Stir in dry pudding mix. Pour over crust.

BAKE 1 hour or until center is almost set. Cool in pan on wire rack. Refrigerate 4 hours or overnight. Lift cheesecake out of pan with foil handles; place on serving platter. Spread with **COOL WHIP**; top with fruit.

Makes 24 servings.

Fruit Pizza

Prep: 25 min. • Bake: 14 min.

1 pkg. (20 oz.) refrigerated sliceable sugar cookies, sliced

1 pkg. (8 oz.) **PHILADELPHIA** Cream Cheese, softened

¼ cup sugar

½ tsp. vanilla

Assorted fruit, such as sliced kiwi, strawberries, blueberries and drained, canned mandarin orange segments

¼ cup apricot preserves, pressed through sieve to remove lumps

1 Tbsp. water

PREHEAT oven to 375°F. Line 12-inch pizza pan with foil; spray with cooking spray. Arrange cookie dough slices in single layer in prepared pan; press together to form crust. Bake 14 min.; cool. Invert onto serving plate; carefully remove foil. Invert on large serving plate or tray so crust is right-side-up.

BEAT cream cheese, sugar and vanilla with electric mixer on medium speed until well blended. Spread over crust.

ARRANGE fruit over cream cheese layer. Mix preserves and water; brush over fruit. Refrigerate 2 hours. Cut into 12 wedges to serve. Store leftover dessert in refrigerator.

Makes 12 servings, 1 wedge each.

"Fruit Smoothie" No-Bake Cheesecake

Prep: 15 min. plus refrigerating

2 cups HONEY MAID Graham Cracker Crumbs

6 Tbsp. butter, melted

3 Tbsp. sugar

4 pkg. (8 oz. each) PHILADELPHIA Neufchâtel Cheese, softened

¾ cup sugar

1 pkg. (12 oz.) frozen mixed berries (strawberries, raspberries, blueberries and blackberries), thawed, drained

1 tub (8 oz.) COOL WHIP LITE Whipped Topping, thawed

LINE 13×9-inch baking pan with foil, with ends of foil extending over sides of pan. Mix graham crumbs, butter and 3 Tbsp. sugar; press firmly onto bottom of prepared pan. Refrigerate while preparing filling.

BEAT Neufchâtel cheese and ¾ cup sugar in large bowl with electric mixer on medium speed until well blended. Add drained berries; beat on low speed just until blended. Gently stir in whipped topping. Spoon over crust; cover.

REFRIGERATE 4 hours or until firm. Use foil handles to remove cheesecake from pan before cutting into pieces to serve. Garnish as desired. Store leftover cheesecake in refrigerator.

Makes 16 servings, 1 piece each.

VARIATION: Omit mixed frozen berries. Add 3 cups fresh mixed berries and additional ¼ cup sugar to Neufchâtel cheese mixture, mixing with electric mixer on medium speed until well blended.

Tiramisu Bowl

Prep: 20 min. plus refrigerating

1 pkg. (8 oz.) **PHILADELPHIA** Cream Cheese, softened

3 cups cold milk

2 pkg. (4-serving size each) **JELL-O** Vanilla Flavor Instant Pudding & Pie Filling

1 tub (8 oz.) **COOL WHIP** Whipped Topping, thawed, divided

48 **NILLA** Wafers, divided

½ cup brewed strong **MAXWELL HOUSE** Coffee, cooled, divided

2 squares **BAKER'S** Semi-Sweet Chocolate, coarsely grated, divided

1 cup fresh raspberries

BEAT cream cheese in large bowl with electric mixer until creamy. Gradually beat in milk. Add dry pudding mixes; mix well. Stir in 2 cups of the whipped topping.

LINE bottom and sides of a 2½-qt. bowl with half of the wafers; drizzle with half of the coffee. Layer half of the pudding mixture over wafers, and then top with half of the grated chocolate. Repeat all layers starting with the wafers and coffee. Top with remaining whipped topping and raspberries.

REFRIGERATE at least 2 hours. Store leftovers in refrigerator.

Makes 16 servings, about ⅔ cup each.

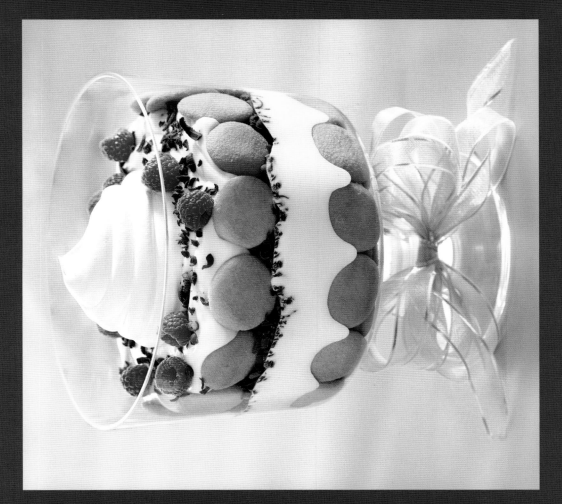

Key Lime Cheesecake Pie

Prep: 25 min. ● Bake: 10 min.

1¼ cups finely crushed coconut bar cookies

¼ cup butter or margarine, melted

3 Tbsp. sugar

2 pkg. (8 oz. each) **PHILADELPHIA** Cream Cheese, softened

1 can (14 oz.) sweetened condensed milk

½ tsp. grated lime peel

⅓ cup lime juice

Few drops green food coloring (optional)

PREHEAT oven to 350°F. Mix cookie crumbs, butter and sugar; press firmly onto bottom and up side of 9-inch pie plate. Bake 10 min. Cool.

BEAT cream cheese and sweetened condensed milk in large bowl with electric mixer on medium speed until well blended. Add peel, juice and food coloring, if desired; mix well. Pour into crust.

REFRIGERATE at least 8 hours or overnight. Store leftover pie in refrigerator.

Makes 10 servings.

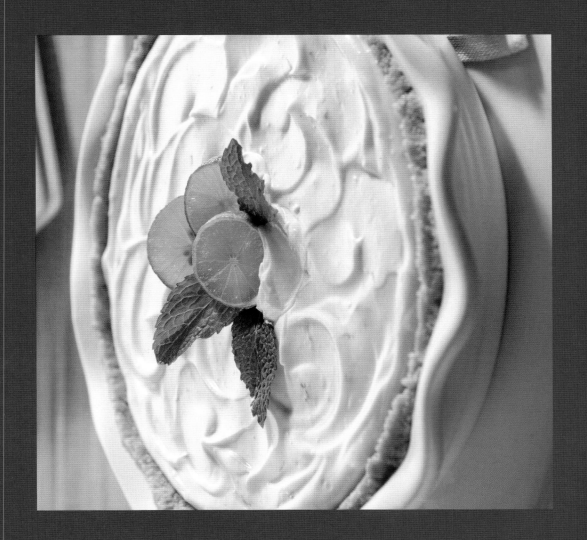

Summer Berry Trifle

Prep: 40 min. plus refrigerating

1 cup boiling water

1 pkg. (8-serving size) JELL-O Strawberry Flavor Gelatin

Ice cubes

½ cup cold water

2 cups mixed berries (raspberries, blueberries, strawberries)

1 pkg. (8 oz.) PHILADELPHIA Cream Cheese, softened

1¼ cups cold milk, divided

1 pkg. (4-serving size) JELL-O Cheesecake or Vanilla Flavor Instant Pudding & Pie Filling

1 tub (6 oz.) COOL WHIP Whipped Topping, thawed

1 pkg. (12 oz.) pound cake, cubed, divided

STIR boiling water into dry gelatin in large bowl at least 2 min. until completely dissolved. Add enough ice to cold water to measure 1 cup. Add to gelatin; stir until ice is completely melted. Let stand about 15 min. or until thickened. (Spoon drawn through gelatin leaves definite impression.) Stir in berries.

PLACE cream cheese in large bowl; beat with wire whisk until creamy. Gradually add ¼ cup of the milk, beating until well blended. Add remaining 1 cup milk and dry pudding mix; beat 2 min. or until well blended. Gently stir in **COOL WHIP**. Set aside.

PLACE about half of the cake cubes in bottom of large serving bowl; cover with half of the pudding mixture. Top with layers of the gelatin mixture, remaining cake cubes and remaining pudding mixture. Refrigerate at least 1 hour. Garnish as desired. Store leftover dessert in refrigerator.

Makes 18 servings.

Orange Grove Mini Cheesecakes

Prep: 20 min. • Bake: 25 min.

24 NILLA Wafers, divided

2 pkg, (8 oz. each) **PHILADELPHIA** Cream Cheese, softened

¼ cup sugar

½ cup BREAKSTONE'S or KNUDSEN Sour Cream

Grated peel from 1 large orange (about 1 Tbsp.)

1 tsp. vanilla

2 eggs

2 squares BAKER'S White Chocolate, melted

¼ cup seedless raspberry preserves, heated

PREHEAT oven to 325°F.

PLACE 1 wafer in each of 12 paper-lined medium muffin cups. Beat cream cheese and sugar in large bowl with electric mixer on medium speed until well blended. Add sour cream, orange peel and vanilla; mix well. Add eggs, 1 at a time, beating on low speed after each addition just until blended. Spoon evenly into prepared muffin cups.

BAKE 20 to 25 min. or until centers are almost set. Cool. Refrigerate 4 hours or overnight. Meanwhile, drizzle chocolate evenly over remaining 12 wafers. Let stand at room temperature until chocolate is firm.

TOP each cheesecake with 1 tsp. preserves and 1 decorated wafer just before serving. Store leftover cheesecakes in refrigerator.

Makes 12 servings, 1 mini cheesecake each.

SIZE-WISE: With their built-in portion control, these mini cheesecakes make a great treat.

SUBSTITUTE: Prepare as directed, using grated lemon peel.

OREO Fruit "Tart"

Prep: 15 min.

1 pkg. (8 oz.) **PHILADELPHIA** Cream Cheese, softened

¼ cup sugar

2 cups thawed **COOL WHIP** Whipped Topping

1 **OREO** Pie Crust (6 oz.)

2 cups assorted fresh fruit pieces (sliced strawberries, raspberries, blueberries and sliced bananas)

4 **OREO** Cookies, finely chopped

2 Tbsp. apricot preserves, melted

BEAT cream cheese and sugar in medium bowl with electric mixer on medium speed 1 min. or until well blended. Gently stir in whipped topping.

SPREAD into pie crust. Top with fruit and chopped cookies; brush fruit with preserves.

REFRIGERATE until ready to serve. Store leftover tart in refrigerator.

Makes 8 servings.

HEALTHY LIVING: To make a reduced-fat version of this tasty dessert, and save 30 calories per serving too, prepare as directed using **PHILADELPHIA** Neufchâtel Cheese, COOL WHIP LITE Whipped Topping and OREO Reduced Fat Cookies.

Mini Strawberry Cheesecakes

Prep: 15 min. plus freezing

1 pkg. (8 oz.) **PHILADELPHIA** Neufchâtel Cheese, softened

1 pkg. (3.4 oz.) **JELL-O** Strawberry Crème Flavor Instant Pudding

1 cup cold fat-free milk

2 cups thawed **COOL WHIP LITE** Whipped Topping

24 **NILLA Wafers, divided**

1 cup sliced fresh strawberries

BEAT Neufchâtel with mixer until creamy. Blend in dry pudding mix. Gradually beat in milk. Stir in **COOL WHIP.**

PLACE 1 wafer on bottom of each of 24 (2-inch) paper baking cups; place in muffin pan. Cover with pudding mixture.

FREEZE 1 hour. Top with berries just before serving.

Makes 24 servings, 1 mini cheesecake each.

HOW TO SOFTEN NEUFCHÂTEL CHEESE: Place completely unwrapped package of Neufchâtel in microwaveable bowl. Microwave on **HIGH 10** sec. or just until softened. **Add 15** sec. for each additional package of Neufchâtel.

Tropical Cheesecake

Prep: 25 min. plus refrigerating

1 pkg. (8 oz.) **PHILADELPHIA Cream Cheese, softened**

⅓ **cup sugar**

1 **tub (8 oz.) COOL WHIP Whipped Topping, thawed**

2 **kiwis, peeled, quartered, sliced and divided**

1 **medium mango, peeled, chopped and divided**

1 cup **BAKER'S ANGEL FLAKE Coconut, toasted, divided**

1 **HONEY MAID** Graham Pie Crust (6 oz.)

BEAT cream cheese and sugar in large bowl with wire whisk or electric mixer until well blended.

ADD whipped topping; stir gently until well blended. Reserve ¼ cup each kiwi, mango and coconut for garnish. Stir remaining kiwi, mango and coconut into cream cheese mixture. Spoon into crust.

REFRIGERATE 3 hours or until set. Top with reserved mango, kiwi and coconut. Store leftover cheesecake in refrigerator.

Makes 8 servings.

SIZE-WISE: Looking for something sweet? One serving of this easy-to-make dessert works well for an after-meal treat.

HOW TO TOAST COCONUT: Place coconut in small nonstick skillet. Cook on medium heat until lightly toasted, stirring frequently.

Layered Pineapple-Lemon Cheesecake Pie

Prep: 15 min. plus refrigerating

1 pkg. (8 oz.) **PHILADELPHIA** Cream Cheese, softened

¼ cup sugar

2 cups thawed **COOL WHIP** Whipped Topping

1 can (8 oz.) crushed pineapple, drained, divided

1 **HONEY MAID** Graham Pie Crust (6 oz.)

1 pkg. (3.4 oz.) **JELL-O** Lemon Flavor Instant Pudding

1⅓ cups cold milk

BEAT cream cheese and sugar in large bowl with whisk until well blended. Stir in **COOL WHIP** and half the pineapple.

SPREAD into crust.

BEAT pudding mix and milk in medium bowl with whisk 2 min. (Mixture will be thick.) Stir in remaining pineapple. Spoon over pie. Refrigerate several hours or until chilled.

Makes 10 servings.

HEALTHY LIVING: Save 90 calories and 8 grams of fat per serving by preparing with PHILADELPHIA Neufchâtel Cheese, COOL WHIP LITE Whipped Topping, a ready-to-use reduced-fat graham cracker crumb crust, fat-free milk and JELL-O Vanilla Flavor Fat Free Sugar Free Instant Pudding.

SUBSTITUTE: Prepare using a NILLA Pie Crust.

Quick & Easy Desserts

PHILADELPHIA No-Bake
Chocolate Cherry Cheesecake

Prep: 10 min. plus refrigerating

2 pkg. (8 oz. each) **PHILADELPHIA** Cream Cheese, softened

1 pkg. (4 oz.) **BAKER'S GERMAN'S** Sweet Chocolate, melted, cooled

⅓ cup sugar

1 tub (8 oz.) **COOL WHIP** Whipped Topping, thawed

1 **HONEY MAID** Graham Pie Crust (6 oz.)

1 can (21 oz.) cherry pie filling

BEAT cream cheese, chocolate and sugar in large bowl with electric mixer on medium speed until well blended. Gently stir in whipped topping.

SPOON into crust.

REFRIGERATE 3 hours or overnight. Top with pie filling just before serving. Store leftover cheesecake in refrigerator.

Makes 10 servings.

PHILADELPHIA 3-STEP Luscious Lemon Cheesecake

Prep: 10 min. • Bake: 40 min.

2 pkg. (8 oz. each) **PHILADELPHIA** Cream Cheese, softened

½ cup sugar

½ tsp. grated lemon peel

1 Tbsp. fresh lemon juice

½ tsp. vanilla

2 eggs

1 **HONEY MAID** Graham Pie Crust (6 oz.)

PREHEAT oven to 350°F. Beat cream cheese, sugar, lemon peel, lemon juice and vanilla with electric mixer on medium speed until well blended. Add eggs; mix just until blended.

POUR into crust.

BAKE 40 min. or until center is almost set. Cool. Refrigerate at least 4 hours. Garnish as desired. Store leftover cheesecake in refrigerator.

Makes 8 servings.

PHILADELPHIA 3-STEP
Key Lime Cheesecake

Prep: 10 min. • Bake: 40 min.

2 pkg. (8 oz. each) **PHILADELPHIA** Cream Cheese, softened

½ cup sugar

1 tsp. grated lime peel

2 Tbsp. fresh lime juice

½ tsp. vanilla

2 eggs

1 **HONEY MAID** Graham Pie Crust (6 oz.)

1 cup thawed **COOL WHIP** Whipped Topping

PREHEAT oven to 350°F. Beat cream cheese, sugar, lime peel, lime juice and vanilla with electric mixer on medium speed until well blended. Add eggs; mix just until blended.

POUR into crust.

BAKE 40 min. or until center is almost set. Cool. Refrigerate 3 hours or overnight. Top with whipped topping just before serving. Garnish as desired. Store leftover cheesecake in refrigerator.

Makes 8 servings.

Chocolate-Berry No-Bake Cheesecake

Prep: 15 min. plus refrigerating

2 squares **BAKER'S** Semi-Sweet Chocolate

2 pkg. (8 oz. each) **PHILADELPHIA** Cream Cheese, softened

⅓ cup sugar

2 cups thawed **COOL WHIP** Chocolate Whipped Topping

1 **OREO** Pie Crust (6 oz.)

1½ cups quartered strawberries

MICROWAVE chocolate in small microwaveable bowl on HIGH 1 min.; stir until chocolate is completely melted. Set aside.

BEAT cream cheese and sugar in large bowl with electric mixer on medium speed until well blended. Add chocolate; mix well. Gently stir in whipped topping. Spoon into crust.

REFRIGERATE 3 hours or until set. Top with strawberries just before serving. Store leftover cheesecake in refrigerator.

Makes 10 servings.

Rocky Road No-Bake Cheesecake

Prep: 15 min. plus refrigerating

3 squares **BAKER'S** Semi-Sweet Chocolate, divided

2 pkg. (8 oz. each) **PHILADELPHIA** Cream Cheese, softened

⅓ cup sugar

¼ cup milk

2 cups thawed **COOL WHIP** Whipped Topping

¾ cup **JET-PUFFED** Miniature Marshmallows

⅓ cup chopped **PLANTERS COCKTAIL** Peanuts

1 **OREO** Pie Crust (6 oz.)

MICROWAVE 1 of the chocolate squares in small microwaveable bowl on HIGH 1 min.; stir until chocolate is completely melted. Set aside.

BEAT cream cheese, sugar and milk in large bowl with electric mixer on medium speed until well blended. Add melted chocolate; mix well. Gently stir in whipped topping, marshmallows and peanuts. Coarsely chop remaining 2 chocolate squares; stir into cream cheese mixture. Spoon into crust.

REFRIGERATE 4 hours or until set. Garnish as desired. Store leftover cheesecake in refrigerator.

Makes 10 servings, 1 slice each.

PHILADELPHIA 3-STEP Cheesecake

Prep: 10 min. • Bake: 40 min.

2 pkg. (8 oz. each) PHILADELPHIA Cream Cheese, softened

½ cup sugar

½ tsp. vanilla

2 eggs

1 HONEY MAID Graham Pie Crust (6 oz.)

PREHEAT oven to 325°F. Beat cream cheese, sugar and vanilla with electric mixer on medium speed until well blended. Add eggs; mix just until blended.

POUR into crust.

BAKE 40 min. or until center is almost set. Cool. Refrigerate 3 hours or overnight. Garnish as desired. Store leftover cheesecake in refrigerator.

Makes 8 servings.

PHILADELPHIA 3-STEP
Coconut Cheesecake

Prep: 10 min. • Bake: 40 min.

2 pkg. (8 oz. each) PHILADELPHIA Cream Cheese, softened

½ cup cream of coconut

½ cup sugar

½ tsp. vanilla

2 eggs

1 HONEY MAID Graham Pie Crust (6 oz.)

2 cups thawed COOL WHIP Whipped Topping

½ cup **BAKER'S ANGEL FLAKE** Coconut, toasted

PREHEAT oven to 350°F. Beat cream cheese, cream of coconut, sugar and vanilla with electric mixer on medium speed until well blended. Add eggs; mix just until blended.

POUR into crust.

BAKE 40 min. or until center is almost set. Cool. Refrigerate 3 hours or overnight. Top with whipped topping and toasted coconut just before serving. Store leftover cheesecake in refrigerator.

Makes 10 servings.

PHILADELPHIA 3-STEP White Chocolate Raspberry Swirl Cheesecake

Prep: 10 min. ● Bake: 40 min.

2 pkg. (8 oz. each) **PHILADELPHIA** Cream Cheese, softened

½ cup sugar

½ tsp. vanilla

2 eggs

3 squares **BAKER'S** White Chocolate, melted

1 **OREO** Pie Crust (6 oz.)

3 Tbsp. raspberry preserves

PREHEAT oven to 350°F. Beat cream cheese, sugar and vanilla with electric mixer on medium speed until well blended. Add eggs; mix just until blended. Stir in white chocolate. Pour into crust.

MICROWAVE preserves in small bowl on HIGH 15 sec. or until melted. Dot top of cheesecake with small spoonfuls of preserves. Cut through batter with knife several times for marble effect.

BAKE 35 to 40 min. or until center is almost set. Cool. Refrigerate 3 hours or overnight. Store leftover cheesecake in refrigerator.

Makes 8 servings.

PHILADELPHIA 3-STEP
Chocolate Chip Cheesecake

Prep: 10 min. ● Bake: 40 min.

2 pkg. (8 oz. each) PHILADELPHIA Cream Cheese, softened

½ cup sugar

½ tsp. vanilla

2 eggs

¾ cup miniature semi-sweet chocolate chips, divided

1 HONEY MAID Graham Pie Crust (6 oz.)

PREHEAT oven to 350°F. Beat cream cheese, sugar and vanilla in large bowl with electric mixer on medium speed until well blended. Add eggs; mix just until blended. Stir in ½ cup of the chips.

POUR into crust. Sprinkle with remaining ¼ cup chips.

BAKE 40 min. or until center is almost set. Cool. Refrigerate 3 hours or overnight. Store leftover cheesecake in refrigerator.

Makes 8 servings.

PHILADELPHIA 3-STEP Cookie Dough Cheesecake

Prep: 10 min. • Bake: 40 min.

2 pkg. (8 oz. each) **PHILADELPHIA** Cream Cheese, softened

½ cup sugar

½ tsp. vanilla

2 eggs

¾ cup prepared or refrigerated chocolate chip cookie dough, divided

1 **HONEY MAID** Graham Pie Crust (6 oz.)

PREHEAT oven to 350°F. Beat cream cheese, sugar and vanilla in large bowl with electric mixer on medium speed until well blended. Add eggs; mix just until blended. Remove ½ cup of the dough; drop by teaspoonfuls into batter. Stir gently.

POUR into crust. Top with level teaspoonfuls of the remaining ¼ cup cookie dough.

BAKE 40 min. or until center is almost set. Cool. Refrigerate 3 hours or overnight. Garnish as desired. Store leftover cheesecake in refrigerator.

Makes 12 servings.

PHILADELPHIA 3-STEP
Double Chocolate Layer Cheesecake

Prep: 10 min. ● Bake: 40 min.

- **2** pkg. (8 oz. each) **PHILADELPHIA** Cream Cheese, softened
- **½** cup sugar
- **½** tsp. vanilla
- **2** eggs
- **3** squares **BAKER'S** Semi-Sweet Chocolate, melted, cooled slightly
- **1** **OREO** Pie Crust (6 oz.)
- **½** cup thawed **COOL WHIP** Whipped Topping
- **4** fresh strawberries, halved

PREHEAT oven to 350°F. Beat cream cheese, sugar and vanilla in large bowl with electric mixer on medium speed until well blended. Add eggs, 1 at a time, beating on low speed after each addition just until blended.

REMOVE 1 cup of the batter to small bowl; stir in melted chocolate. Pour into crust; top with remaining plain batter.

BAKE 40 min. or until center is almost set. Cool. Refrigerate 3 hours or overnight. Top with whipped topping and strawberries just before serving. Store leftover cheesecake in refrigerator.

Makes 8 servings.

PHILADELPHIA 3-STEP Double Layer Pumpkin Cheesecake

Prep: 10 min. • Bake: 40 min.

- **2 pkg. (8 oz. each) PHILADELPHIA Cream Cheese, softened**
- ½ **cup sugar**
- ½ **tsp. vanilla**
- **2 eggs**
- ½ **cup canned pumpkin**
- ½ **tsp. ground cinnamon**
-   **Dash ground cloves**
-   **Dash ground nutmeg**
- **1 HONEY MAID Graham Pie Crust (6 oz.)**

PREHEAT oven to 325°F. Beat cream cheese, sugar and vanilla with electric mixer on medium speed until well blended. Add eggs, 1 at a time, mixing on low speed after each addition just until blended. Remove 1 cup of the batter; stir in pumpkin and spices.

POUR remaining plain batter into crust. Top with pumpkin batter.

BAKE 40 min. or until center is almost set. Cool. Refrigerate 3 hours or overnight. Garnish as desired. Store leftover cheesecake in refrigerator.

Makes 8 servings.

PHILADELPHIA Blueberry No-Bake Cheesecake

Prep: 15 min. plus refrigerating

2 cups **HONEY MAID** Graham Cracker Crumbs

6 Tbsp. margarine, melted

1 cup sugar, divided

4 pkg. (8 oz. each) **PHILADELPHIA** Neufchâtel Cheese, softened

½ cup blueberry preserves

Grated peel from 1 lemon

1 pkg. (16 oz.) frozen blueberries, thawed, drained

1 tub (8 oz.) **COOL WHIP LITE** Whipped Topping, thawed

MIX graham crumbs, margarine and ¼ cup of the sugar; press firmly onto bottom of 13×9-inch pan. Refrigerate while preparing filling.

BEAT Neufchâtel cheese and remaining ¾ cup sugar in large bowl with electric mixer on medium speed until well blended. Add preserves and lemon peel, mix until blended. Stir in blueberries. Gently stir in whipped topping. Spoon over crust; cover.

REFRIGERATE 4 hours or until firm. Garnish as desired. Store leftovers in refrigerator.

Makes 16 servings, 1 piece each.

HOW TO MAKE IT WITH FRESH BLUEBERRIES: Place 2 cups blueberries in small bowl with 2 Tbsp. sugar; mash with fork. Add to Neufchâtel cheese mixture; continue as directed.

PHILADELPHIA White Chocolate Raspberry No-Bake Cheesecake

Prep: 15 min. plus refrigerating

30 Reduced Fat OREO Chocolate Sandwich Cookies

¼ cup margarine, melted

4 pkg. (8 oz. each) PHILADELPHIA Neufchâtel Cheese, softened

¾ cup sugar

½ cup raspberry fruit spread

1 pkg. (12 oz.) frozen raspberries, thawed, drained

1 tub (8 oz.) COOL WHIP LITE Whipped Topping, thawed

1 square BAKER'S White Chocolate, shaved

PLACE cookies in food processor; cover. Process 30 to 45 sec. or until finely ground. Add margarine; mix well. Press firmly onto bottom of 13×9-inch pan. Refrigerate while preparing filling.

BEAT Neufchâtel cheese and sugar in large bowl with electric mixer on medium speed until well blended. Add fruit spread; mix well. Stir in raspberries. Gently stir in whipped topping. Spoon over crust; cover.

REFRIGERATE 4 hours or until firm. Top with shaved chocolate just before serving. Store leftovers in refrigerator.

Makes 16 servings, 1 piece each.

HOW TO MAKE IT WITH FRESH RASPBERRIES: Place 2 cups raspberries in small bowl with 2 Tbsp. sugar; mash with fork. Add to Neufchâtel cheese mixture; continue as directed.

CHIPS AHOY! Cheesecake Sandwiches

Prep: 10 min. plus freezing

4 oz. (½ of 8-oz. pkg.) **PHILADELPHIA** Cream Cheese, softened

2 Tbsp. sugar

1 cup thawed **COOL WHIP** Whipped Topping

20 **CHIPS AHOY!** Real Chocolate Chip Cookies

1 tub (7 oz.) **BAKER'S Real Milk Dipping Chocolate, melted**

BEAT cream cheese and sugar in large bowl with electric mixer on medium speed until well blended. Stir in whipped topping.

COVER bottom (flat) side of each of 10 of the cookies with about 2 Tbsp. of the cream cheese mixture; top each with second cookie, bottom-side down, to form sandwich. Dip half of each sandwich in melted chocolate; gently shake off excess chocolate. Place in single layer in airtight container.

FREEZE 3 hours or until firm. Store leftover sandwiches in freezer.

Makes 10 servings, 1 sandwich each.

Creamy Strawberry Cookie "Tarts"

Prep: 15 min. plus refrigerating

⅔ cup boiling water

1 pkg. (4-serving size) **JELL-O** Strawberry Flavor Gelatin

1 pkg. (8 oz.) **PHILADELPHIA** Cream Cheese, cubed

1 cup thawed **COOL WHIP** Whipped Topping

12 **CHIPS AHOY!** Real Chocolate Chip Cookies

12 small sliced strawberries

STIR boiling water into dry gelatin mix in small bowl at least 2 min. until completely dissolved. Cool 5 min., stirring occasionally.

POUR gelatin mixture into blender. Add cream cheese; cover. Blend on medium speed 30 to 45 sec. or until well blended; scrape down side of blender container, if needed. Add whipped topping; cover. Blend on low speed 5 sec. or just until blended.

LINE 12 muffin pan cups with paper liners; spray with cooking spray. Place 1 cookie on bottom of each prepared cup; top evenly with the gelatin mixture. Refrigerate 1 hour 30 min. or until firm. Top each with a strawberry just before serving. Store leftover desserts in refrigerator.

Makes 12 servings.

Strawberry Cheesecake Squares

Prep: 15 min. plus refrigerating

30 NILLA Wafers, finely crushed (about 1 cup)

3 Tbsp. butter or margarine, melted

2 Tbsp. sugar

⅓ cup strawberry jam

1 pkg. (8 oz.) PHILADELPHIA Cream Cheese, softened

⅓ cup sugar

1 tub (8 oz.) COOL WHIP Whipped Topping, thawed

8 strawberries, halved

MIX wafer crumbs, butter and 2 Tbsp. sugar in small bowl with fork. Press firmly onto bottom of foil-lined 8-inch square pan. Carefully spread jam over crust.

BEAT cream cheese and ⅓ cup sugar in large bowl with wire whisk or electric mixer on medium speed until well blended. Gently stir in whipped topping; spoon over crust.

REFRIGERATE 3 hours or until set. Cut into 16 squares. Top each square with strawberry half. Store leftover dessert in refrigerator.

Makes 16 servings, 1 square each.

PHILADELPHIA 3-STEP
Low-Fat Berry Cheesecake

Prep: 10 min. ● Bake: 45 min.

3 pkg. (8 oz. each) PHILADELPHIA Fat Free Cream Cheese, softened

¾ cup sugar

1 tsp. grated lemon peel

1 Tbsp. fresh lemon juice

½ tsp. vanilla

3 eggs

¼ cup crushed HONEY MAID Low Fat Honey Grahams

½ cup sliced strawberries

½ cup blueberries

½ cup raspberries

2 Tbsp. strawberry jelly, melted

PREHEAT oven to 300°F. Beat cream cheese, sugar, lemon peel, lemon juice and vanilla with electric mixer on medium speed until well blended. Add eggs, 1 at a time, mixing on low speed after each addition just until blended. Spray 9-inch pie plate with cooking spray; sprinkle bottom with graham crumbs.

POUR cream cheese mixture into prepared pie plate.

BAKE 45 min. or until center is almost set. Cool. Refrigerate 3 hours or overnight. Top with fruit; drizzle with jelly.

Makes 10 servings.

Fluffy 2-STEP Cheesecake Minis

Prep: 10 min. plus refrigerating

12 **NILLA** Wafers

1 pkg. (8 oz.) **PHILADELPHIA** Cream Cheese, softened

⅓ cup sugar

1 tub (8 oz.) **COOL WHIP** Whipped Topping, thawed, divided

¼ cup **BAKER'S ANGEL FLAKE** Coconut, toasted

PLACE 1 wafer on bottom of each of 12 paper-lined medium muffin cups; set aside. Beat cream cheese and sugar in large bowl with wire whisk or electric mixer until well blended. Add 2¼ cups of the whipped topping; mix well. Spoon evenly into muffin cups.

REFRIGERATE 3 hours or overnight. Spread tops with remaining whipped topping. Sprinkle with coconut just before serving. Store leftover cheesecakes in refrigerator.

Makes 1 dozen or 12 servings, 1 cheesecake each.

OREO No-Bake Cheesecake

Prep: 15 min. plus refrigerating

1 pkg. (1 lb. 2 oz.) **OREO Chocolate Sandwich Cookies, divided**

¼ cup **butter, melted**

4 pkg. (8 oz. each) **PHILADELPHIA Cream Cheese, softened**

½ cup sugar

1 tsp. vanilla

1 tub (8 oz.) **COOL WHIP Whipped Topping, thawed**

LINE 13×9-inch pan with foil, with ends of foil extending over sides of pan. Coarsely chop 15 of the cookies; set aside. Finely crush remaining cookies; mix with butter. Press firmly onto bottom of prepared pan. Refrigerate while preparing filling.

BEAT cream cheese, sugar and vanilla in large bowl with electric mixer on medium speed until well blended. Gently stir in whipped topping and chopped cookies. Spoon over crust; cover.

REFRIGERATE 4 hours or until firm. Store leftover cheesecake in refrigerator.

Makes 24 servings, 1 piece each.

VARIATION: Prepare as directed, using 1 pkg. (18 oz.) Golden Uh-Oh! OREO Chocolate Creme Sandwich Cookies.

Fluffy Cheesecake

Prep: 15 min. plus refrigerating

1 pkg. (8 oz.) **PHILADELPHIA** Cream Cheese, softened

⅓ cup sugar

1 tub (8 oz.) **COOL WHIP** Whipped Topping, thawed

1 **HONEY MAID** Graham Pie Crust (6 oz.)

1 apple, cored, thinly sliced

BEAT cream cheese and sugar in large bowl with wire whisk or electric mixer until well blended. Gently stir in whipped topping.

SPOON into crust.

REFRIGERATE 3 hours or until set. Top with apple slices just before serving.

Makes 8 servings.

FLUFFY CHEESECAKE SQUARES: Omit pie crust. Mix 1 cup **HONEY MAID** Graham Cracker Crumbs, 2 Tbsp. sugar and ⅓ cup melted butter or margarine. Press onto bottom of foil-lined 8-inch square pan. Continue as directed. **Makes 9 servings.**

FLUFFY CHERRY CHEESECAKE: Prepare and refrigerate as directed. Top with 1½ cups cherry pie filling just before serving.

PHILADELPHIA 3-STEP Mini Cheesecakes

Prep: 10 min. • Bake: 20 min.

2 pkg. (8 oz. each) **PHILADELPHIA** Cream Cheese, softened

½ cup sugar

½ tsp. vanilla

2 eggs

12 **OREO** Chocolate Sandwich Cookies

1 kiwi, peeled, cut into 6 slices

36 blueberries (about ½ cup)

12 raspberries (about ⅓ cup)

PREHEAT oven to 350°F. Beat cream cheese, sugar and vanilla in large bowl with electric mixer on medium speed until well blended. Add eggs, 1 at a time, beating on low speed after each addition just until blended.

PLACE 1 cookie in bottom of each of 12 medium paper-lined muffin cups. Fill evenly with batter.

BAKE 20 min. or until centers are almost set. Cool. Refrigerate 3 hours or overnight. Cut kiwi slices in half. Top each cheesecake with 1 kiwi half, 3 blueberries and 1 raspberry just before serving.

Makes 12 servings.

CHEESECAKE SQUARES: Line 8-inch square baking pan with foil. Mix 1½ cups finely crushed OREO Chocolate Sandwich Cookies or **HONEY MAID** Honey Grahams with ¼ cup melted butter; press firmly onto bottom of pan. Prepare cheesecake batter as directed. Pour over crust. Bake and refrigerate as directed. Cut into 16 squares. Top evenly with the fruit mixture just before serving. Makes 16 servings, 1 square each.

PHILADELPHIA Chocolate
Cheesecakes for Two

Prep: 10 min. plus refrigerating

2 oz. (¼ of 8-oz. pkg.) **PHILADELPHIA** Cream Cheese, softened

1 Tbsp. sugar

1 square **BAKER'S** Semi-Sweet Chocolate, melted

½ cup thawed **COOL WHIP** Whipped Topping

2 **OREO** Chocolate Sandwich Cookies

BEAT cream cheese, sugar and chocolate in medium bowl with wire whisk until well blended. Add whipped topping; mix well.

PLACE 1 cookie on bottom of each of 2 paper-lined medium muffin cups; fill evenly with cream cheese mixture.

REFRIGERATE 2 hours or overnight. (Or, if you are in a hurry, place in the freezer for 1 hour.)

Makes 2 servings.

SPECIAL EXTRA: Dust surface of chilled cheesecake with unsweeteened cocoa powder just before serving. Top with heart-shaped stencil; dust with powdered sugar. Remove stencil.

S'mores Cheesecake Squares

Prep: 20 min. • Bake: 40 min.

18 **HONEY MAID** Honey Grahams, divided

⅓ cup butter or margarine, melted

3 Tbsp. sugar

4 pkg. (8 oz. each) **PHILADELPHIA** Cream Cheese, softened

1 cup sugar

1 Tbsp. vanilla

3 Tbsp. flour

4 eggs

1 cup **BAKER'S** Semi-Sweet Chocolate Chunks, divided

1 cup **JET-PUFFED** Miniature Marshmallows

PREHEAT oven to 350°F.

LINE 13×9-inch baking pan with foil, with ends of foil extending over sides of pan. Crush 14 of the grahams. (You should have about 2 cups crumbs.) Mix graham crumbs, butter and 3 Tbsp. sugar; press firmly onto bottom of prepared pan. Coarsely chop remaining 4 grahams; set aside.

BEAT cream cheese, 1 cup sugar and the vanilla in large bowl with electric mixer on medium speed until well blended. Add flour; mix well. Add eggs, 1 at a time, mixing on low speed after each addition just until blended. Chop ½ cup of the chocolate chunks; stir into cream cheese mixture. Pour over crust. Sprinkle with remaining ½ cup chocolate chunks, the marshmallows and reserved chopped grahams.

BAKE 40 min. or until center is almost set. Cool completely. Cover. Refrigerate 4 hours or overnight. Remove cheesecake from pan using foil handles before cutting into squares to serve. Store any leftover cheesecake in refrigerator.

Makes 32 servings, 1 square each.

SUBSTITUTE: Prepare as directed, using PHILADELPHIA Neufchâtel Cheese.

Chocolate-Covered OREO Cookie Cake

Prep: 20 min. plus baking and cooling

1 pkg. (2-layer size) devil's food chocolate cake mix

4 squares **BAKER'S** Semi-Sweet Chocolate

¼ cup butter

1 pkg. (8 oz.) **PHILADELPHIA** Cream Cheese, softened

½ cup sugar

2 cups thawed **COOL WHIP** Whipped Topping

12 **OREO** Cookies, coarsely crushed

PREHEAT oven to 350°F.

PREPARE cake batter and bake in 2 (9-inch) round pans as directed on package. Cool cakes in pans 10 min. Invert cakes onto wire racks; gently remove pans. Cool cakes completely.

MICROWAVE chocolate and butter in small microwaveable bowl on HIGH 2 min. or until butter is melted. Stir until chocolate is completely melted. Cool 5 min.

MEANWHILE, beat cream cheese and sugar in large bowl with mixer until blended. Gently stir in **COOL WHIP** and crushed cookies. Stack cake layers on plate, spreading cream cheese mixture between layers. Spread top with chocolate glaze; let stand until firm. Keep refrigerated.

Makes 16 servings.

FAMILY FUN: This great-tasting cake looks like a giant OREO Cookie.

COOKING KNOW-HOW: If chocolate glaze becomes too thick, microwave on HIGH 20 to 30 sec. or until of desired consistency.

SIZE-WISE: Enjoy a serving of this indulgent cake on occasion, but keep portion size in mind. One cake makes enough for 16 servings.

Frozen Coconut Pie

Prep: 15 min. plus freezing

4 oz. (½ of 8-oz. pkg.) **PHILADELPHIA** Cream Cheese, softened

1 Tbsp. sugar

½ cup milk

1 cup **BAKER'S ANGEL FLAKE** Coconut

1 tub (8 oz.) **COOL WHIP** or **COOL WHIP** Extra Creamy Whipped Topping, thawed

½ tsp. almond or vanilla extract

1 **HONEY MAID** Graham Pie Crust (6 oz.)

BEAT cream cheese and sugar in large bowl with electric mixer on medium speed until well blended. Gradually add milk, beating until well blended after each addition.

STIR in coconut, whipped topping and extract. Spoon into crust.

FREEZE 4 hours or until firm. Remove pie from freezer about 15 min. before serving. Let stand at room temperature until pie can be cut easily. Store leftover pie in freezer.

Makes 8 servings.

SIZE-WISE: Enjoy a serving of this rich and indulgent treat on special occasions.

USE YOUR BLENDER: Place cream cheese, sugar and milk in blender container; cover. Blend on low speed 30 sec.; spoon into medium bowl. Gently stir in coconut, whipped topping and extract. Spoon into crust and continue as directed.

HOW TO SOFTEN CREAM CHEESE: Place completely unwrapped package of cream cheese in microwaveable bowl. Microwave on HIGH 10 sec. or just until softened. Add 15 sec. for each additional package of cream cheese.

Candy Bar Pie

Prep: 20 min. plus refrigerating

- **4** oz. (½ of 8-oz. pkg.) **PHILADELPHIA Cream Cheese**, softened
- **1** Tbsp. milk
- **1** tub (12 oz.) **COOL WHIP Whipped Topping**, thawed, divided
- **1** (2.07 oz.) chocolate-coated caramel-peanut nougat bar, finely chopped
- **1½** cups cold milk
- **2** pkg. (4-serving size) **JELL-O Chocolate Instant Pudding**
- **1** **OREO Pie Crust (6 oz.)**

MIX cream cheese and 1 Tbsp. milk in large bowl with wire whisk until well blended. Add 1½ cups of the whipped topping and chopped candy bar; stir gently.

POUR 1½ cups cold milk into another large bowl. Add pudding mixes. Beat with wire whisk 2 min. or until well blended. (Mixture will be thick.) Gently stir in 2 cups of the remaining whipped topping. Spread half of the pudding mixture onto bottom of crust; cover with cream cheese mixture. Top with remaining pudding mixture.

REFRIGERATE 4 hours or until set. Garnish with remaining whipped topping. Store leftover pie in refrigerator.

Makes 10 servings.

HEALTHY LIVING: Save 30 calories and 4 grams of fat per serving by preparing with PHILADELPHIA Neufchâtel Cheese, fat-free milk and COOL WHIP LITE Whipped Topping.

HOW TO SOFTEN CREAM CHEESE: Place measured amount of cream cheese in microwaveable bowl. Microwave on HIGH 10 sec. or until slightly softened.

Coffee-Drizzled Cream Cheese Pie

Prep: 15 min. plus refrigerating

1 pkg. (8 oz.) **PHILADELPHIA Cream Cheese, softened**

⅓ cup sugar

¼ cup milk

2 Tbsp. **GENERAL FOODS INTERNATIONAL** Suisse Mocha Café

1 **HONEY MAID** Graham Pie Crust (6 oz.)

1 tub (8 oz.) **COOL WHIP Whipped Topping, thawed**

BEAT cream cheese in medium bowl until creamy. Gradually add sugar, mixing until well blended. Stir in milk. Remove ¼ cup of the cream cheese mixture; place in small bowl. Stir in flavored instant coffee mix. Drizzle 1 Tbsp. of the coffee-flavored cream cheese mixture onto bottom of crust. Set remaining coffee-flavored cream cheese mixture aside.

STIR whipped topping gently into remaining plain cream cheese mixture, stirring just until combined. Spoon into crust. Drizzle with remaining coffee-flavored cream cheese mixture. Swirl knife gently through mixtures several times for marble effect.

REFRIGERATE 2 hours or until set. Store leftover pie in refrigerator.

Makes 8 servings.

SIZE IT UP: Desserts can be part of a balanced diet, but remember to keep tabs on portions.

GREAT SUBSTITUTE: Omit milk. Substitute **1** cup BREAKSTONE'S or KNUDSEN Sour Cream for the cream cheese.

Chocolate Silk Pie with Marshmallow Meringue

Prep: 15 min. plus refrigerating

5 squares **BAKER'S** Bittersweet Chocolate, divided

4 oz. (½ of 8-oz. pkg.) **PHILADELPHIA** Cream Cheese, softened

1 jar (7 oz.) **JET-PUFFED** Marshmallow Creme, divided

1 pkg. (3.9 oz.) **JELL-O** Chocolate Instant Pudding

1 cup milk

1 **OREO** Pie Crust (6 oz.)

1 cup thawed **COOL WHIP** Whipped Topping

MICROWAVE 4 chocolate squares in medium microwaveable bowl on HIGH 1 to 1½ min. or until melted, stirring after 1 min. Add cream cheese, ½ of marshmallow creme, dry pudding mix and milk; beat with mixer until well blended. Spoon into crust.

BEAT remaining marshmallow creme and **COOL WHIP** in separate bowl until well blended. Spread over chocolate layer in crust.

REFRIGERATE 2 hours or until firm. Use remaining chocolate square to make chocolate curls; arrange on pie.

Makes 10 servings.

SIZE-WISE: Since this special-occasion dessert makes enough to feed a crowd, it makes a great dessert to serve at your next party or family gathering.

HOW TO MAKE CHOCOLATE CURLS: Microwave chocolate square on HIGH a few seconds or just until you can smudge chocolate with your thumb. Pull a vegetable peeler slowly along bottom of square to make curl. Repeat to make additional curls.

PHILADELPHIA 3-Step
Strawberry Layer Cheesecake

Prep: 10 min. • Bake: 40 min.

2 pkg. (8 oz. each) **PHILADELPHIA** Cream Cheese, softened

½ cup sugar

½ tsp. vanilla

2 eggs

¼ cup strawberry preserves

5 drops red food coloring

1 **HONEY MAID** Graham Pie Crust (6 oz.)

1 cup thawed **COOL WHIP** Whipped Topping

4 medium strawberries, sliced

PREHEAT oven to 350°F.

BEAT cream cheese, sugar and vanilla with electric mixer on medium speed until well blended. Add eggs; mix just until blended. Remove 1 cup of the batter. Add preserves and food coloring; stir until well blended. Pour into crust; cover with the remaining plain batter.

BAKE 40 min. or until center is almost set. Cool.

REFRIGERATE 3 hours or overnight. Top with whipped topping and strawberries just before serving. Store leftover cheesecake in refrigerator.

Makes 8 servings.

GREAT SUBSTITUTE: Prepare as directed, using a NILLA Pie Crust.

PHILADELPHIA 3-Step
White Chocolate Cheesecake

Prep: 10 min. ● Bake: 35 min.

2 pkg. (8 oz. each) **PHILADELPHIA** Cream Cheese, softened

½ cup sugar

½ tsp. vanilla

2 eggs

4 squares **BAKER'S** White Chocolate, chopped, divided

1 **OREO** Pie Crust (6 oz.)

16 candy-coated almonds

PREHEAT oven to 350°F.

BEAT cream cheese, sugar and vanilla in large bowl with electric mixer on medium speed until well blended. Add eggs; mix just until blended. Stir in half of the white chocolate.

POUR into crust. Sprinkle with remaining white chocolate.

BAKE 35 min. or until center is almost set. Cool. Refrigerate 3 hours or overnight. Top with almonds just before serving. Store leftover cheesecake in refrigerator.

Makes 8 servings.

SIZE-WISE: Enjoy a serving of this rich and indulgent cheesecake on a special occasion.

PLAIN CHEESECAKE: Prepare as directed, omitting white chocolate and substituting HONEY MAID Graham Pie Crust for the OREO Pie Crust.

CHOCOLATE CHEESECAKE: Prepare as directed, substituting **4** squares BAKER'S Semi-Sweet Chocolate, melted, for the white chocolate. Stir melted chocolate into batter after mixing in eggs.

PHILADELPHIA 3-Step Pina Colada Cheesecake

Prep: 10 min. • Bake: 40 min.

2 pkg. (8 oz. each) **PHILADELPHIA** Cream Cheese, softened

½ cup sugar

½ tsp. vanilla

2 eggs

⅓ cup thawed frozen pina colada tropical fruit mixer concentrate

1 **HONEY MAID** Graham Pie Crust (6 oz.)

4 canned pineapple rings, drained and sliced

¼ cup **BAKER'S ANGEL FLAKE** Coconut

PREHEAT oven to 350°F.

BEAT cream cheese, sugar and vanilla with electric mixer on medium speed until well blended. Add eggs; mix just until blended. Stir in fruit mixer concentrate.

POUR into crust.

BAKE 40 min. or until center is almost set. Cool. Refrigerate at least 3 hours before serving. Top with pineapple and coconut. Store leftover cheesecake in refrigerator.

Makes 8 servings.

SIZE IT UP: Keep an eye on portion size when you enjoy this rich dessert!

STRAWBERRY DAIQUIRI CHEESECAKE: Prepare as directed, using frozen strawberry daiquiri concentrate. Garnish with fresh strawberries just before serving.

LIME MARGARITA CHEESECAKE: Prepare as directed, using frozen margarita concentrate. Garnish with lime slices just before serving.

PHILADELPHIA QUICK & EASY DESSERTS

PHILADELPHIA 3-Step
Lemon Cheesecake Bars

Prep: 10 min. • Bake: 25 min.

- 1½ cups soft coconut macaroon cookie crumbs
- 2 Tbsp. margarine, melted
- 2 pkg. (8 oz. each) PHILADELPHIA Cream Cheese, softened
- ½ cup sugar
- ½ tsp. grated lemon peel
- 1 Tbsp. fresh lemon juice
- ½ tsp. vanilla
- 2 eggs

PREHEAT oven to 350°F.

MIX cookie crumbs and margarine. Press firmly onto bottom of greased 8-inch square baking pan.

BEAT cream cheese, sugar, lemon peel, lemon juice and vanilla in large bowl with electric mixer on medium speed until well blended. Add eggs, 1 at a time, beating just until blended after each addition. Pour over crust.

BAKE 20 to 25 min. or until center is almost set. Cool. Refrigerate at least 3 hours or overnight. Cut into bars to serve. Store leftover bars in refrigerator.

Makes 16 servings, 1 bar each.

JAZZ IT UP: Sprinkle with additional grated lemon peel just before serving.

HOW TO EASILY REMOVE BARS FROM PAN: Line pan with foil, with ends of foil extending over sides of pan, before pressing crumb mixture onto bottom of pan. Use foil handles to remove chilled cheesecake from pan before cutting into bars to serve.

PHILADELPHIA 3-Step
Coconut Cheesecake Bars

Prep: 10 min. ● Bake: 25 min.

1½ cups soft coconut macaroon cookie crumbs

2 Tbsp. margarine, melted

2 pkg. (8 oz. each) **PHILADELPHIA** Cream Cheese, softened

½ cup sugar

½ cup cream of coconut

½ tsp. vanilla

2 eggs

PREHEAT oven to 350°F.

MIX cookie crumbs and margarine. Press firmly onto bottom of greased 8-inch square baking pan; set aside. Beat cream cheese, sugar, cream of coconut and vanilla in large bowl with electric mixer on medium speed until well blended. Add eggs; beat just until blended.

POUR over crust.

BAKE 20 to 25 min. or until center is almost set. Cool. Refrigerate 3 hours or overnight. Cut into 16 bars to serve. Store leftover bars in refrigerator.

Makes 16 servings, 1 bar each.

SIZE IT UP: Enjoy a serving, 1 bar, of this rich dessert on occasion.

HOW TO EASILY REMOVE BARS FROM PAN: Line pan with foil, with ends of foil extending over sides of pan. Grease foil. Press crumb mixture onto bottom of pan and continue as directed. After dessert is baked and cooled, lift from pan, using foil handles. Discard foil. Cut into bars as directed.

Classic Cheesecakes

White Chocolate Cheesecake

Prep: 30 min. • Bake: 1 hour

¾ cup sugar, divided

½ cup butter, softened

1½ tsp. vanilla, divided

1 cup flour

4 pkg. (8 oz. each) **PHILADELPHIA** Cream Cheese, softened

2 pkg. (6 squares each) **BAKER'S** White Chocolate, melted, slightly cooled

4 eggs

1 pt. (2 cups) raspberries

PREHEAT oven to 325°F if using a silver 9-inch springform pan (or to 300°F if using a dark nonstick 9-inch springform pan). Beat ¼ cup of the sugar, the butter and ½ tsp. of the vanilla in small bowl with electric mixer on medium speed until light and fluffy. Gradually add flour, mixing on low speed until well blended after each addition. Press firmly onto bottom of pan; prick with fork. Bake 25 min. or until edge is lightly browned.

BEAT cream cheese, remaining ½ cup sugar and remaining 1 tsp. vanilla in large bowl with electric mixer on medium speed until well blended. Add melted chocolate; mix well. Add eggs, 1 at a time, beating on low speed after each addition just until blended. Pour over crust.

BAKE 55 min. to 1 hour or until center is almost set. Run knife or metal spatula around rim of pan to loosen cake; cool before removing rim of pan. Refrigerate 4 hours or overnight. Top with the raspberries just before serving. Store leftover cheesecake in refrigerator.

Makes 16 servings.

Ribbon Bar Cheesecake

Prep: 15 min. ● Bake: 40 min.

30 **OREO** Chocolate Sandwich Cookies, crushed

½ cup butter, melted

¼ cup **PLANTERS** Chopped Pecans

¼ cup **BAKER'S ANGEL FLAKE** Coconut

4 pkg. (8 oz. each) **PHILADELPHIA** Cream Cheese, softened

1 cup sugar

4 eggs

½ cup whipping cream

6 squares **BAKER'S** Semi-Sweet Chocolate

PREHEAT oven to 350°F. Mix crushed cookies, butter, pecans and coconut; press firmly onto bottom of 13×9-inch baking pan. Refrigerate while preparing filling.

BEAT cream cheese and sugar in large bowl with electric mixer on medium speed until well blended. Add eggs, 1 at a time, mixing on low speed after each addition just until blended. Pour over crust.

BAKE 40 min. or until center is almost set. Cool. Refrigerate 3 hours or overnight. Place whipping cream and chocolate in saucepan. Cook on low heat until chocolate is completely melted and mixture is well blended, stirring occasionally. Pour over cheesecake. Refrigerate 15 min. or until chocolate is firm. Store leftover cheesecake in refrigerator

Makes 16 servings, 1 square each.

Boston Cream Cheesecake

Prep: 35 min. • Bake: 45 min.

1 pkg. (1-layer size) yellow cake mix

3 pkg. (8 oz. each) **PHILADELPHIA** Cream Cheese, softened

¾ cup granulated sugar

2 tsp. vanilla, divided

¾ cup **BREAKSTONE'S** or **KNUDSEN** Sour Cream

3 eggs

2 squares **BAKER'S** Unsweetened Chocolate

3 Tbsp. milk

2 Tbsp. butter or margarine

1 cup powdered sugar

PREHEAT oven to 325°F. Grease bottom of 9-inch springform pan. Prepare cake batter as directed on package; pour into prepared pan. Bake 25 min, if using a silver springform pan. (Bake at 300°F for 20 min. if using a dark nonstick springform pan.) Cool.

BEAT cream cheese, granulated sugar and 1 tsp. of the vanilla in large bowl with electric mixer on medium speed until well blended. Add sour cream; mix well. Add eggs, 1 at a time, mixing on low speed after each addition just until blended. Pour over cake layer in pan.

BAKE 40 to 45 min. or until center is almost set if using a silver springform pan. (Bake at 300°F for 40 to 45 min. or until center is almost set if using a dark nonstick springform pan.) Run knife or metal spatula around rim of pan to loosen cake; cool before removing rim of pan.

PLACE chocolate, milk and butter in medium microwaveable bowl. Microwave on HIGH 2 min. or until butter is melted, stirring after 1 min. Stir until chocolate is completely melted. Add powdered sugar and remaining 1 tsp. vanilla; mix well. Spread over cooled cheesecake. Refrigerate 4 hours or overnight.

Makes 16 servings.

Marbled White Chocolate Cheesecake

Prep: 15 min. • Bake: 40 min.

1½ cups crushed **FAMOUS** Chocolate Wafers

3 Tbsp. butter or margarine, melted

3 pkg. (8 oz. each) **PHILADELPHIA** Cream Cheese, softened

½ cup sugar

½ tsp. vanilla

3 eggs

2 squares **BAKER'S** Semi-Sweet Chocolate, melted

1 pkg. (6 squares) **BAKER'S** White Chocolate, melted

PREHEAT oven to 350°F if using a silver 9-inch springform pan (or to 325°F if using a dark nonstick 9-inch springform pan). Mix crushed wafers and butter. Press firmly onto bottom of pan. Bake 10 min.

BEAT cream cheese, sugar and vanilla in large bowl with electric mixer on medium speed until well blended. Add eggs, 1 at a time, mixing on low speed after each addition just until blended. Remove 1 cup of the cream cheese mixture; place in small bowl. Add melted semi-sweet chocolate; stir until well blended. Add melted white chocolate to remaining cream cheese mixture; mix well. Spoon semi-sweet and white chocolate mixtures alternately over crust. Swirl with knife to marbleize.

BAKE 40 min. or until center is almost set. Run small knife or spatula around side of pan to loosen cake; cool before removing rim of pan. Refrigerate 4 hours or overnight. Store leftover cheesecake in refrigerator.

Makes 12 servings.

PHILADELPHIA New York Cheesecake

Prep: 15 min. • Bake: 40 min.

1 cup crushed **HONEY MAID** Honey Grahams (about 6 grahams)

3 Tbsp. sugar

3 Tbsp. butter or margarine, melted

5 pkg. (8 oz. each) **PHILADELPHIA** Cream Cheese, softened

1 cup sugar

3 Tbsp. flour

1 Tbsp. vanilla

1 cup **BREAKSTONE'S** or **KNUDSEN** Sour Cream

4 eggs

1 can (21 oz.) cherry pie filling

PREHEAT oven to 325°F. Mix graham crumbs, 3 Tbsp. sugar and butter; press firmly onto bottom of 13×9-inch baking pan. Bake 10 min.

BEAT cream cheese, 1 cup sugar, flour and vanilla with electric mixer on medium speed until well blended. Add sour cream; mix well. Add eggs, 1 at a time, mixing on low speed after each addition just until blended. Pour over crust.

BAKE 40 min. or until center is almost set. Cool completely. Refrigerate at least 4 hours or overnight. Top with pie filling before serving. Store leftover cheesecake in refrigerator.

Makes 16 servings, 1 slice each.

PHILLY OREO Cheesecake

Prep: 20 min. ● Bake: 40 min.

1 pkg. (1 lb. 2 oz.) **OREO Chocolate Sandwich Cookies, divided**

¼ cup butter or margarine, melted

4 pkg. (8 oz. each) **PHILADELPHIA Cream Cheese, softened**

1 cup sugar

1 tsp. vanilla

1 cup **BREAKSTONE'S** or **KNUDSEN Sour Cream**

4 eggs

PREHEAT oven to 325°F. Line 13×9-inch baking pan with foil, with ends of foil extending over sides of pan. Place 30 of the cookies in food processor; cover. Process 30 to 45 sec. or until finely ground. Add butter; mix well. Press firmly onto bottom of prepared pan.

BEAT cream cheese, sugar and vanilla in large bowl with electric mixer on medium speed until well blended. Add sour cream; mix well. Add eggs, 1 at a time, beating just until blended after each addition. Chop remaining cookies. Gently stir 1½ cups of the chopped cookies into cream cheese batter. Pour over crust; sprinkle with the remaining chopped cookies.

BAKE 40 min. or until center is almost set. Cool. Refrigerate 4 hours or overnight. Lift cheesecake from pan, using foil handles. Cut into 16 pieces to serve. Store leftover cheesecake in refrigerator.

Makes 16 servings, 1 piece each.

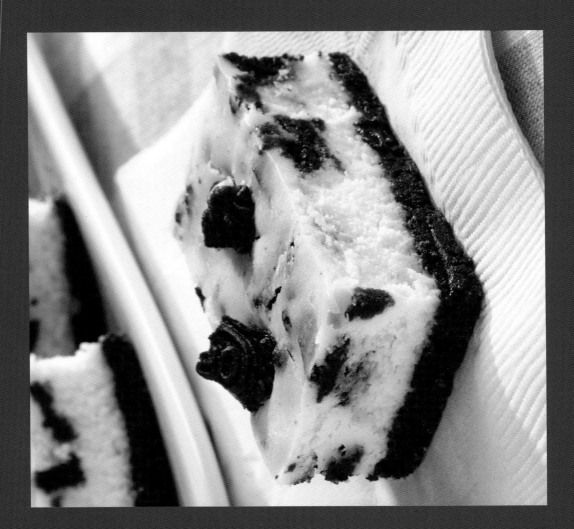

PHILLY Brownie Cheesecake

Prep: 15 min. • Bake: 40 min.

1 pkg. (19 to 21 oz.) brownie mix (13×9-inch pan size)

4 pkg. (8 oz. each) PHILADELPHIA Cream Cheese, softened

1 cup sugar

1 tsp. vanilla

½ cup BREAKSTONE'S or KNUDSEN Sour Cream

3 eggs

2 squares BAKER'S Semi-Sweet Chocolate

PREHEAT oven to 325°F. Spray 13×9-inch baking pan with cooking spray. Prepare brownie batter as directed on package; pour into prepared pan. Bake 25 min. or until top of brownie is shiny and center is almost set.

MEANWHILE, beat cream cheese, sugar and vanilla in large bowl with electric mixer on medium speed until well blended. Add sour cream; mix well. Add eggs, 1 at a time, mixing on low speed after each addition just until blended. Gently pour over brownie layer in pan. (Filling will come almost to top of pan.)

BAKE 40 min. or until center is almost set. Run knife or metal spatula around rim of pan to loosen side of dessert from pan; cool. Refrigerate at least 4 hours or overnight.

MELT chocolate as directed on package; drizzle over cheesecake. Refrigerate 15 min. or until chocolate is firm. Cut cheesecake into 16 pieces to serve. Store any leftover cheesecake in refrigerator.

Makes 16 servings, 1 piece each.

PHILADELPHIA Chocolate-Vanilla Swirl Cheesecake

Prep: 15 min. ● Bake: 40 min.

20 **OREO** Chocolate Sandwich Cookies, crushed (about 2 cups)

3 Tbsp. butter, melted

4 pkg. (8 oz. each) **PHILADELPHIA** Cream Cheese, softened

1 cup sugar

1 tsp. vanilla

1 cup **BREAKSTONE'S** or **KNUDSEN** Sour Cream

4 eggs

6 squares **BAKER'S** Semi-Sweet Chocolate, melted, cooled

PREHEAT oven to 325°F. Line 13×9-inch baking pan with foil, with ends of foil extending over sides of pan. Mix cookie crumbs and butter; press firmly onto bottom of prepared pan. Bake 10 min.

BEAT cream cheese, sugar and vanilla in large bowl with electric mixer on medium speed until well blended. Add sour cream; mix well. Add eggs, 1 at a time, beating on low speed after each addition just until blended. Remove 1 cup of the batter; set aside. Stir melted chocolate into remaining batter in large bowl; pour over crust. Top with spoonfuls of the remaining 1 cup plain batter; cut through batters with knife several times for swirled effect.

BAKE 40 min. or until center is almost set. Cool. Refrigerate at least 4 hours or overnight. Use foil handles to lift cheesecake from pan before cutting to serve. Garnish as desired. Store leftovers in refrigerator.

Makes 16 servings, 1 piece each.

Caramel-Pecan Cheesecake Bars

Prep: 15 min. • Bake: 40 min.

½ cup **NABISCO** Graham Cracker Crumbs

1 cup coarsely chopped **PLANTERS** Pecans, divided

2 Tbsp. granulated sugar

¼ cup butter, melted

4 pkg. (8 oz. each) **PHILADELPHIA** Cream Cheese, softened

1 cup firmly packed brown sugar

2 Tbsp. flour

½ cup **BREAKSTONE'S** or **KNUDSEN** Sour Cream

1 Tbsp. vanilla

3 eggs

1 bag (14 oz.) **KRAFT** Caramels, divided

2 Tbsp. water, divided

PREHEAT oven to 350°F. Line 13×9-inch baking pan with foil, with ends of foil extending over sides of pan. Mix graham crumbs, ½ cup pecans, granulated sugar and butter; press firmly onto bottom of prepared pan. Bake 10 min.

BEAT cream cheese, brown sugar and flour in large bowl with electric mixer on medium speed until well blended. Add sour cream and vanilla; mix well. Add eggs, 1 at a time, mixing on low speed after each addition just until blended. Place 36 of the caramels and 1 Tbsp. water in microwaveable bowl. Microwave on HIGH 1 min. or until caramels are completely melted when stirred. Add to cream cheese batter; stir until well blended. Pour over crust.

BAKE 40 min. or until center is almost set. Sprinkle cheesecake with remaining ½ cup pecans. Refrigerate at least 4 hours or overnight.

PLACE remaining caramels and additional 1 Tbsp. water in microwaveable bowl. Microwave on HIGH 1 min. or until caramels are completely melted when stirred. Drizzle over cheesecake; let stand until set. Remove dessert from pan using foil handles; cut into 32 bars to serve. Store leftover bars in refrigerator.

Makes 32 servings, 1 bar each.

Pumpkin Swirl Cheesecake

Prep: 20 min. • Bake: 1 hour 5 min.

25 NABISCO Ginger Snaps, finely crushed (about 1½ cups)

½ cup finely chopped **PLANTERS** Pecans

¼ cup butter, melted

4 pkg. (8 oz. each) **PHILADELPHIA** Cream Cheese, softened

1 cup sugar, divided

1 tsp. vanilla

4 eggs

1 cup canned pumpkin

1 tsp. ground cinnamon

¼ tsp. ground nutmeg

Dash ground cloves

PREHEAT oven to 325°F if using a silver 9-inch springform pan (or to 300°F if using a dark nonstick 9-inch springform pan). Mix ginger snap crumbs, pecans and butter; press onto bottom and 1 inch up side of pan.

BEAT cream cheese, ¾ cup of the sugar and the vanilla with electric mixer until well blended. Add eggs, 1 at a time, mixing on low speed after each addition just until blended. Remove 1½ cups of the batter; place in small bowl. Stir remaining ¼ cup sugar, the pumpkin and spices into remaining batter. Spoon half of the pumpkin batter into crust; top with spoonfuls of half of the reserved plain batter. Repeat layers. Cut through batters with knife several times for marble effect.

BAKE 55 min. to 1 hour 5 min. or until center is almost set. (Test doneness by gently shaking the pan. If the cheesecake is done, it will be set except for an approximately 2½-inch area in the center that will be soft and jiggly.) Run knife or metal spatula around rim of pan to loosen cake; cool before removing rim. Refrigerate at least 4 hours or overnight. Store leftovers in refrigerator.

Makes 16 servings, 1 piece each.

Chocolate Royale Cheesecake Squares

Prep: 20 min. ● Bake: 50 min.

24 **OREO** Chocolate Sandwich Cookies, crushed (about 2 cups)

¼ cup butter or margarine, melted

4 pkg. (8 oz. each) **PHILADELPHIA** Cream Cheese, softened

1 cup sugar

2 Tbsp. flour

1 tsp. vanilla

1 pkg. (8 squares) **BAKER'S** Semi-Sweet Chocolate, melted, slightly cooled

4 eggs

PREHEAT oven to 325°F. Mix cookie crumbs and butter; press firmly onto bottom of 13×9-inch baking pan. Bake 10 min.

BEAT cream cheese, sugar, flour and vanilla in large bowl with electric mixer on medium speed until well blended. Add melted chocolate; mix well. Add eggs, 1 at a time, mixing on low speed after each addition just until blended. Pour over crust.

BAKE 45 to 50 min. or until center is almost set. Refrigerate at least 4 hours or overnight. Cut into 32 squares to serve. Store leftover dessert squares in refrigerator.

Makes 32 servings, 1 square each.

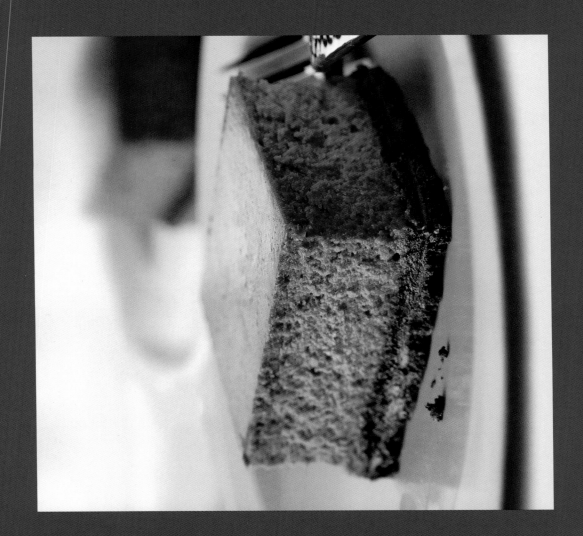

CLASSIC CHEESECAKES

PHILADELPHIA New York-Style
Strawberry Swirl Cheesecake

Prep: 15 min. • Bake: 40 min.

1 cup **HONEY MAID** Graham Cracker Crumbs

3 Tbsp. sugar

3 Tbsp. butter, melted

5 pkg. (8 oz. each) **PHILADELPHIA** Cream Cheese, softened

1 cup sugar

3 Tbsp. flour

1 Tbsp. vanilla

1 cup **BREAKSTONE'S** or **KNUDSEN** Sour Cream

4 eggs

⅓ cup seedless strawberry jam

PREHEAT oven to 325°F. Line 13×9-inch baking pan with foil, with ends of foil extending over sides of pan. Mix cracker crumbs, 3 Tbsp. sugar and the butter; press firmly onto bottom of prepared pan. Bake 10 min.

BEAT cream cheese, 1 cup sugar, the flour and vanilla in large bowl with electric mixer on medium speed until well blended. Add sour cream; mix well. Add eggs, 1 at a time, mixing on low speed after each addition just until blended. Pour over crust. Gently drop small spoonfuls of jam over batter; cut through batter several times with knife for marble effect.

BAKE 40 min. or until center is almost set. Cool completely. Refrigerate at least 4 hours or overnight. Lift cheesecake from pan using foil handles. Cut into 16 pieces to serve. Store leftover cheesecake in refrigerator.

Makes 16 servings, 1 piece each.

PHILLY Blueberry Swirl Cheesecake

Prep: 15 min. ● Bake: 45 min.

1 cup **HONEY MAID** Graham Cracker Crumbs

1 cup plus 3 Tbsp. sugar, divided

3 Tbsp. butter or margarine, melted

4 pkg. (8 oz. each) **PHILADELPHIA** Cream Cheese, softened

1 tsp. vanilla

1 cup **BREAKSTONE'S** or **KNUDSEN** Sour Cream

4 eggs

2 cups fresh or thawed frozen blueberries

PREHEAT oven to 325°F. Mix graham crumbs, 3 Tbsp. of the sugar and the butter. Press firmly onto bottom of foil-lined 13×9-inch baking pan. Bake 10 min.

BEAT cream cheese, remaining 1 cup sugar and the vanilla in large bowl with electric mixer on medium speed until well blended. Add sour cream; mix well. Add eggs, 1 at a time, beating on low speed after each addition just until blended. Pour over crust. Purée the blueberries in a blender or food processor. Gently drop spoonfuls of the puréed blueberries over batter; cut through batter several times with knife for marble effect.

BAKE 45 min. or until center is almost set; cool. Refrigerate at least 4 hours or overnight. Garnish as desired. Store leftover cheesecake in refrigerator.

Makes 16 servings.

New York-Style Sour Cream-Topped Cheesecake

Prep: 15 min. • Bake: 50 min.

1½ cups **HONEY MAID** Graham Cracker Crumbs

¼ cup butter, melted

1¼ cups sugar, divided

4 pkg. (8 oz. each) **PHILADELPHIA** Cream Cheese, softened

2 tsp. vanilla, divided

1 container (16 oz.) **BREAKSTONE'S** or **KNUDSEN** Sour Cream, divided

4 eggs

PREHEAT oven to 325°F. Line 13×9-inch baking pan with foil, with ends of foil extending over sides of pan. Mix graham crumbs, butter and 2 Tbsp. of the sugar; press firmly onto bottom of prepared pan.

BEAT cream cheese, 1 cup of the remaining sugar and 1 tsp. of the vanilla in large bowl with electric mixer on medium speed until well blended. Add 1 cup of the sour cream; mix well. Add eggs, 1 at a time, beating on low speed after each addition just until blended. Pour over crust.

BAKE 40 min. or until center is almost set. Mix remaining sour cream, 2 Tbsp. sugar and 1 tsp. vanilla until well blended; carefully spread over cheesecake. Bake an additional 10 min. Cool. Cover; refrigerate 4 hours or overnight. Lift cheesecake from pan, using foil handles. Garnish as desired. Store leftover cheesecake in refrigerator.

Makes 16 servings, 1 piece each.

PHILADELPHIA White Chocolate-Peppermint Cheesecake

Prep: 15 min. ● Bake: 40 min.

1½ cups **HONEY MAID** Graham Cracker Crumbs

3 Tbsp. sugar

¼ cup butter, melted

4 pkg. (8 oz. each) **PHILADELPHIA** Cream Cheese, softened

1 cup sugar

¼ tsp. peppermint extract

1 cup **BREAKSTONE'S** or **KNUDSEN** Sour Cream

4 squares **BAKER'S** White Chocolate, melted

4 eggs

1 cup thawed **COOL WHIP** Whipped Topping

16 miniature candy canes

PREHEAT oven to 325°F. Line 13×9-inch baking pan with foil, with ends of foil extending over sides of pan. Mix graham crumbs, 3 Tbsp. sugar and the butter; press firmly onto bottom of prepared pan. Bake 10 min.

BEAT cream cheese, 1 cup sugar and the extract in large bowl with electric mixer on medium speed until well blended. Add sour cream and chocolate; mix well. Add eggs, 1 at a time, mixing on low speed after each addition just until blended. Pour over crust.

BAKE 40 min. or until center is almost set. Cool. Refrigerate at least **4** hours or overnight. Lift cheesecake from pan, using foil handles. Top each piece with a dollop of the whipped topping and a candy cane just before serving. Store any leftover cheesecake in refrigerator.

Makes 16 servings, 1 piece each.

Tiramisu Cheesecake

Prep: 20 min. • Bake: 45 min.

1 box (12 oz.) **NILLA** Wafers (about 88 wafers), divided

5 tsp. **MAXWELL HOUSE** Instant Coffee, divided

3 Tbsp. hot water, divided

4 pkg. (8 oz. each) **PHILADELPHIA** Cream Cheese, softened

1 cup sugar

1 cup **BREAKSTONE'S** or **KNUDSEN** Sour Cream

4 eggs

1 cup thawed **COOL WHIP** Whipped Topping

2 Tbsp. unsweetened cocoa powder

PREHEAT oven to 325°F. Line 13×9-inch baking pan with foil, with ends of foil extending over sides of pan. Layer half of the wafers (about 44) on bottom of prepared pan. Dissolve 2 tsp. of the coffee granules in 2 Tbsp. of the hot water. Brush wafers with half of the dissolved coffee mixture; set remaining aside.

BEAT cream cheese and sugar in large bowl with electric mixer on medium speed until well blended. Add sour cream; mix well. Add eggs, 1 at a time, mixing on low speed after each addition just until blended. Dissolve remaining 3 tsp. coffee granules in remaining 1 Tbsp. hot water. Remove 3½ cups of the batter; place in medium bowl. Stir in dissolved coffee. Pour coffee-flavored batter over wafers in baking pan. Layer remaining wafers over batter. Brush wafers with reserved dissolved coffee. Pour remaining plain batter over wafers.

BAKE 45 min. or until center is almost set. Cool. Refrigerate 3 hours or overnight. Lift cheesecake from pan, using foil handles. Spread with whipped topping; sprinkle with cocoa. Cut into 16 pieces to serve. Store leftover cheesecake in refrigerator.

Makes 16 servings, 1 piece each.

German Chocolate Cheesecake

Prep: 30 min. ● Bake: 50 min.

1 cup finely crushed **FAMOUS** Chocolate Wafers

1 cup sugar, divided

3 Tbsp. butter or margarine, melted

3 pkg. (8 oz. each) **PHILADELPHIA** Cream Cheese, softened

¼ cup flour

1 pkg. (4 oz.) **BAKER'S GERMAN'S** Sweet Chocolate, melted

2½ tsp. vanilla, divided

4 eggs, divided

⅓ cup canned evaporated milk

¼ cup butter or margarine

½ cup **BAKER'S ANGEL FLAKE** Coconut

½ cup **PLANTERS** Chopped Pecans

PREHEAT oven to 350°F.

MIX chocolate wafer crumbs, 2 Tbsp. of the sugar and 3 Tbsp. butter; press firmly onto bottom of 9-inch springform pan. Bake 10 min.

BEAT cream cheese, ½ cup of the sugar and the flour in large bowl with electric mixer on medium speed until well blended. Add chocolate and 2 tsp. of the vanilla; mix well. Add 3 of the eggs, 1 at a time, mixing on low speed after each addition just until blended. Pour over crust.

BAKE 45 to 50 min. or until center is almost set. Run knife or metal spatula around rim of pan to loosen cake; cool before removing rim of pan. Refrigerate 4 hours or overnight.

PLACE milk, remaining sugar, the ¼ cup butter, remaining egg and remaining ½ tsp. vanilla in small saucepan; cook on medium-low heat until thickened, stirring constantly. Stir in coconut and pecans. Cool. Spread over cheesecake just before serving. Store leftover cheesecake in refrigerator.

Makes 14 servings.

PHILADELPHIA Blueberry Crown Cheesecake

Prep: 15 min. ● Bake: 1 hour 15 min.

PREHEAT oven to 325°F.

30 **NILLA Wafers**, crushed (about 1 cup)

1 cup plus 3 Tbsp. sugar, divided

3 Tbsp. butter or margarine, melted

5 pkg. (8 oz. each) **PHILADELPHIA** Cream Cheese, softened

3 Tbsp. flour

1 Tbsp. vanilla

Grated peel from 1 medium lemon

1 cup **BREAKSTONE'S** or **KNUDSEN** Sour Cream

4 eggs

2 cups fresh blueberries

MIX wafer crumbs, 3 Tbsp. of the sugar and butter until well blended. Press firmly onto bottom of 9-inch springform pan.

BEAT cream cheese, remaining 1 cup sugar, flour, vanilla and lemon peel with electric mixer on medium speed until well blended. Add sour cream; mix well. Add eggs, 1 at a time, beating on low speed after each addition just until blended. Pour over crust; top with blueberries.

BAKE 1 hour 10 min. to 1 hour 15 min. or until center is almost set. Run small knife or spatula around rim of pan to loosen cake; cool before removing rim of pan. Refrigerate at least 4 hours before serving. Store leftover cheesecake in refrigerator.

Makes 16 servings.

SIZE IT UP: Savor a serving of this crowd-pleasing dessert on special occasions.

SPECIAL EXTRA: Garnish with additional blueberries and fresh mint sprigs just before serving.

Double-Decker OREO Cheesecake

Prep: 25 min. • Bake: 45 min.

1 pkg. (1 lb. 1 oz.) **OREO** Chocolate Creme Chocolate Sandwich Cookies (48 cookies), divided

¼ cup butter, melted

4 pkg. (8 oz. each) **PHILADELPHIA** Cream Cheese, softened

1 cup sugar

1 tsp. vanilla

1 cup **BREAKSTONE'S** or **KNUDSEN** Sour Cream

4 eggs

4 squares **BAKER'S** Semi-Sweet Chocolate, melted

PREHEAT oven to 325°F.

PROCESS 30 cookies in food processor until finely ground. Add butter; mix well. Press onto bottom of 13×9-inch baking pan.

BEAT cream cheese, sugar and vanilla in large bowl with mixer until well blended. Add sour cream; mix well. Add eggs, 1 at a time, beating after each just until blended; pour half over crust. Stir melted chocolate into remaining batter; pour over batter in pan. Chop remaining cookies; sprinkle over batter.

BAKE 45 min. or until center is almost set. Cool completely. Refrigerate 4 hours

Makes 16 servings.

MAKE AHEAD: Wrap cooled cheesecake tightly in foil. Freeze up to 2 months. Thaw in refrigerator overnight before serving.

HOW TO REMOVE FROM PAN EASILY: Line pan with foil, with ends extending over sides. Prepare as directed. Use foil handles to lift cheesecake from pan before cutting.

Easy Entertaining

Barbecue Bacon Party Spread

Prep: 15 min.

2 pkg. (8 oz. each) **PHILADELPHIA** Cream Cheese, softened

½ cup **KRAFT THICK 'N SPICY** Original Barbecue Sauce

1 pkg. (2.8 oz.) **OSCAR MAYER** Real Bacon Recipe Pieces

1 small tomato, chopped

½ cup chopped green pepper

⅓ cup sliced green onions

1½ cups **KRAFT** Shredded Cheddar Cheese

TRISCUIT Thin Crisps

SPREAD cream cheese on large platter; drizzle with barbecue sauce.

TOP with all remaining ingredients except the Thin Crisps.

SERVE with the Thin Crisps.

Makes 35 servings, 2 Tbsp. spread and 11 Thin Crisps each.

Mexican Layered Dip

Prep: 10 min. plus refrigerating

1 pkg. (8 oz.) **PHILADELPHIA** Neufchâtel Cheese, softened

1 Tbsp. **TACO BELL® HOME ORIGINALS®** Taco Seasoning Mix

1 cup **TACO BELL® HOME ORIGINALS®** Thick 'N Chunky Salsa

1 cup rinsed canned black beans

1 cup shredded lettuce

1 cup **KRAFT** 2% Milk Shredded Cheddar Cheese

4 green onions, chopped

2 Tbsp. sliced black olives

BEAT Neufchâtel with mixer until creamy. Add seasoning mix; mix well. Spread onto bottom of 9-inch pie plate or serving plate.

TOP with remaining ingredients.

REFRIGERATE 1 hour. Serve with assorted cut-up fresh vegetables.

Makes 5 cups or 40 servings, 2 Tbsp. each.

SPECIAL EXTRA: Garnish with chopped fresh cilantro.

TACO BELL® and HOME ORIGINALS® are trademarks owned and licensed by Taco Bell Corp.

EASY ENTERTAINING **PHILADELPHIA**

Cool Veggie Pizza Appetizer

Prep: 20 min. ● Bake: 13 min.

2 cans (8 oz. each) refrigerated crescent dinner rolls

1 pkg. (8 oz.) PHILADELPHIA Cream Cheese, softened

½ cup MIRACLE WHIP Dressing

1 tsp. dill weed

½ tsp. onion salt

1 cup broccoli florets

1 cup chopped green pepper

1 cup chopped seeded tomato

¼ cup chopped red onion

PREHEAT oven to 375°F. Separate dough into 4 rectangles. Press onto bottom and up side of 15 × 10 × 1-inch baking pan to form crust.

BAKE 11 to 13 min. or until golden brown; cool.

MIX cream cheese, dressing, dill and onion salt until well blended. Spread over crust; top with remaining ingredients. Refrigerate. Cut into squares.

Makes 32 servings.

PHILLY Fresh Mediterranean Dip

Prep: 10 min.

1 pkg. (8 oz.) **PHILADELPHIA** Neufchâtel Cheese, softened

½ cup chopped tomato

½ cup cucumbers

½ cup chopped spinach leaves

¼ cup chopped red onions

2 Tbsp. **KRAFT** Greek Vinaigrette Dressing

¼ cup **ATHENOS** Crumbled Feta Cheese with Basil & Tomato

SPREAD Neufchâtel cheese onto bottom of 9-inch pie plate.

MIX remaining ingredients except feta cheese; spoon over Neufchâtel cheese. Sprinkle with feta cheese.

SERVE with **WHEAT THINS** Snack Crackers or assorted cut-up fresh vegetables.

Makes 1¾ cups or 14 servings, 2 Tbsp. each.

PHILLY BBQ Ranch Chicken Dip

Prep: 10 min.

1 pkg. (8 oz.) **PHILADELPHIA** Neufchâtel Cheese, softened

¼ cup **KRAFT** Barbecue Sauce, any flavor

1 pkg. (6 oz.) **OSCAR MAYER** Grilled Chicken Breast Strips, chopped

2 Tbsp. **KRAFT** Light Ranch Reduced Fat Dressing

¼ cup chopped red pepper

¼ cup sliced green onions

SPREAD Neufchâtel cheese onto bottom of microwaveable 9-inch pie plate. Spread barbecue sauce over Neufchâtel cheese. Top with chicken.

MICROWAVE on HIGH 2 min. or until heated through. Top with remaining ingredients.

SERVE with **WHEAT THINS** Snack Crackers and cut-up vegetables.

Makes 2¼ cups or 18 servings, 2 Tbsp. each.

Pecan Tassies

Prep: 20 min. • Bake: 25 min.

4 oz. (½ of 8-oz. pkg.) PHILADELPHIA Cream Cheese, softened

½ cup butter or margarine, softened

1 cup flour

1 egg

¾ cup firmly packed brown sugar

1 tsp. vanilla

¾ cup finely chopped PLANTERS Pecans

3 squares BAKER'S Semi-Sweet Chocolate, melted

BEAT cream cheese and butter in large bowl with electric mixer on medium speed until well blended. Add flour; mix well. Cover and refrigerate at least 1 hour or until chilled.

PREHEAT oven to 350°F. Divide dough into 24 balls. Place 1 ball in each of 24 miniature muffin pan cups; press onto bottoms and up sides of cups to form shells. Set aside. Beat egg lightly in small bowl. Add sugar and vanilla; mix well. Stir in pecans. Spoon evenly into pastry shells, filling each shell three-fourths full.

BAKE 25 min. or until lightly browned. Let stand 5 min. in pans; remove to wire racks. Cool completely. Drizzle with melted chocolate. Let stand until set.

Makes 2 dozen or 24 servings, 1 tart each.

Easy Petit Fours

Prep: 5 min.

¼ cup **PHILADELPHIA** Strawberry Cream Cheese Spread

12 **OREO** White Fudge Covered Chocolate Sandwich Cookies

6 strawberries, halved

1 square **BAKER'S** Semi-Sweet Chocolate, melted

SPREAD 1 tsp. cream cheese onto each cookie. Top each with strawberry half.

DRIZZLE each strawberry-topped cookie with melted chocolate.

Makes 12 servings.

PHILLY Buffalo Chicken Dip

Prep: 10 min.

1 pkg. (8 oz.) **PHILADELPHIA** Cream Cheese, softened

1 pkg. (6 oz.) **OSCAR MAYER** Oven Roasted Chicken Breast Cuts

½ cup **Buffalo wing sauce**

¼ cup **KRAFT** Natural Blue Cheese Crumbles

¼ cup **sliced green onions**

SPREAD cream cheese onto bottom of microwaveable 9-inch pie plate. Mix chicken and sauce; spoon over cream cheese. Sprinkle with blue cheese and onions.

MICROWAVE on HIGH 2 min. or until heated through.

SERVE warm with celery sticks and **WHEAT THINS** Snack Crackers.

Makes 2¼ cups or 18 servings, 2 Tbsp. each.

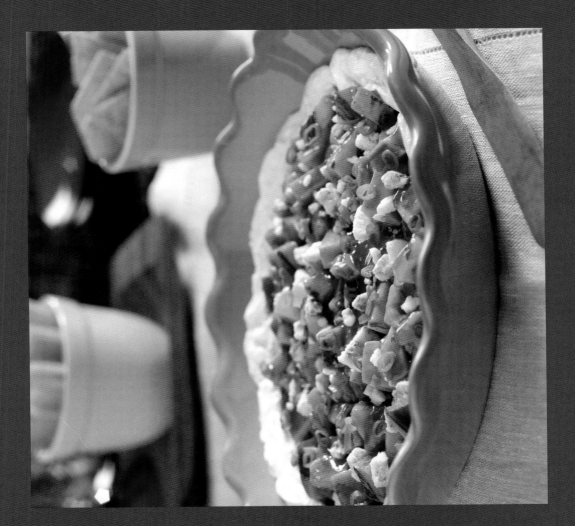

Cream Cheese Nibbles

Prep: 10 min. plus refrigerating

1 pkg. (8 oz.) **PHILADELPHIA** Cream Cheese

½ cup **KRAFT** Sun-Dried Tomato Dressing

2 cloves garlic, sliced

3 small sprigs fresh rosemary, stems removed

6 sprigs fresh thyme, cut into pieces

1 tsp. black peppercorns

Peel of 1 lemon, cut into thin strips

CUT cream cheese into 36 pieces. Place in 9-inch pie plate.

ADD remaining ingredients; toss lightly. Cover.

REFRIGERATE at least 1 hour or up to 24 hours. Serve with crusty bread, **NABISCO** Crackers or pita chips.

Makes 18 servings, 2 pieces each.

Heavenly Ham Roll-Ups

Prep: 15 min. • Bake: 20 min.

1 pkg. (9 oz.) **OSCAR MAYER Shaved Smoked Ham**

5 Tbsp. **PHILADELPHIA Light Cream Cheese Spread**

15 **asparagus spears (about 1 lb.), trimmed**

PREHEAT oven to 350°F. Flatten ham slices; pat dry. Stack ham in piles of 2 slices each; spread each stack with 1 tsp. of the cream cheese spread.

PLACE 1 aparagus spear on one of the long sides of each ham stack; roll up. Place in 13×9-inch baking dish.

BAKE 15 to 20 min. or until heated through.

Makes 15 servings, 1 roll-up each.

PHILLY Cheesy Pizza Dip

Prep: 10 min.

1 pkg. (8 oz.) **PHILADELPHIA** Cream Cheese, softened

½ cup pizza sauce

½ cup **KRAFT** Shredded Mozzarella Cheese

2 Tbsp. **KRAFT** 100% Grated Parmesan Cheese

2 Tbsp. each: chopped red and green peppers

1 tsp. Italian seasoning

RITZ Crackers

SPREAD cream cheese onto bottom of microwaveable 9-inch pie plate. Cover with pizza sauce; top with all remaining ingredients except crackers.

MICROWAVE on HIGH 2 min. or until heated through.

SERVE with the crackers.

Makes 2 cups dip or 16 servings, 2 Tbsp. dip and 5 crackers each.

PHILLY Cheesy Chili Dip

Prep: 5 min.

1 pkg. (8 oz.) **PHILADELPHIA** Cream Cheese, softened

1 can (15 oz.) chili

½ cup **KRAFT** Shredded Cheddar Cheese

2 Tbsp. chopped cilantro

SPREAD cream cheese onto bottom of microwaveable 9-inch pie plate; top with chili and Cheddar cheese.

MICROWAVE on HIGH 45 sec. to 1 min. or until Cheddar cheese is melted. Sprinkle with cilantro.

SERVE with assorted **NABISCO** Crackers.

Makes 3 cups or 24 servings, 2 Tbsp. each.

PHILLY Shrimp Cocktail Dip

Prep: 10 min.

1 pkg. (8 oz.) **PHILADELPHIA** Cream Cheese, softened

¾ lb. cooked shrimp, chopped (about 2 cups)

¾ cup **KRAFT** Cocktail Sauce

¼ cup **KRAFT** Shredded Parmesan Cheese

¼ cup sliced green onions

SPREAD cream cheese onto bottom of 9-inch pie plate. Toss shrimp with cocktail sauce; spoon over cream cheese.

SPRINKLE with Parmesan cheese and onions.

SERVE with **WHEAT THINS** Snack Crackers.

Makes 3 cups or 24 servings, 2 Tbsp. each.

PHILLY Tomato-Basil Dip

Prep: 10 min.

1 pkg. (8 oz.) **PHILADELPHIA Neufchâtel Cheese, softened**

2 plum tomatoes, chopped

2 Tbsp. **KRAFT Zesty Italian Dressing**

2 Tbsp. **KRAFT Shredded Parmesan Cheese**

1 Tbsp. **finely chopped fresh basil**

SPREAD Neufchâtel cheese onto bottom of 9-inch pie plate.

MIX tomatoes and dressing; spoon over Neufchâtel cheese. Sprinkle with Parmesan cheese and basil.

SERVE with **WHEAT THINS** Snack Crackers or assorted cut-up fresh vegetables.

Makes 1¾ cups or 14 servings, 2 Tbsp. each.

PHILADELPHIA Mexican Dip

Prep: 10 min.

1 pkg. (8 oz.) **PHILADELPHIA** Neufchâtel Cheese, softened

½ cup **TACO BELL® HOME ORIGINALS®** Thick 'N Chunky Salsa

½ cup **KRAFT** 2% Milk Shredded Reduced Fat Cheddar Cheese

2 green onions, sliced (about ¼ cup)

WHEAT THINS Reduced Fat Baked Snack Crackers

SPREAD Neufchâtel cheese onto bottom of 9-inch pie plate.

TOP with layers of salsa, Cheddar cheese and onions.

SERVE with the crackers.

Makes 1⅔ cups dip or 13 servings, 2 Tbsp. dip and 16 crackers each.

TACO BELL® and HOME ORIGINALS® are trademarks owned and licensed by Taco Bell Corp.

PHILADELPHIA Garden Vegetable Dip

Prep: 10 min. plus refrigerating

2 pkg. (8 oz. each) **PHILADELPHIA** Cream Cheese, softened

½ cup **KRAFT** Blue Cheese Dressing

½ cup finely chopped broccoli

1 medium carrot, shredded

MIX cream cheese and dressing until well blended. Stir in vegetables; cover.

REFRIGERATE several hours or until chilled.

SERVE with assorted cut-up fresh vegetables.

Makes 20 servings, 2 Tbsp. each.

BLT Dip

Prep: 15 min.

1 pkg. (8 oz.) **PHILADELPHIA** Cream Cheese, softened

¾ cup shredded or chopped romaine lettuce

2 plum tomatoes, seeded, chopped

4 slices **OSCAR MAYER** Bacon, crisply cooked, drained and crumbled

SPREAD cream cheese onto bottom of 9-inch pie plate.

TOP with lettuce and tomatoes; sprinkle with bacon.

SERVE with **WHEAT THINS** Snack Crackers or assorted cut-up fresh vegetables.

Makes 2 cups or 16 servings, 2 Tbsp. each.

Party Cheese Ball

Prep: 15 min. plus refrigerating

- 2 pkg. (8 oz. each) **PHILADELPHIA** Cream Cheese, softened
- 1 pkg. (8 oz.) **KRAFT** Shredded Sharp Cheddar Cheese
- 1 Tbsp. finely chopped onions
- 1 Tbsp. chopped red peppers
- 2 tsp. Worcestershire sauce
- 1 tsp. lemon juice
  Dash ground red pepper (cayenne)
  Dash salt
- 1 cup chopped **PLANTERS** Pecans

BEAT cream cheese and Cheddar cheese in small bowl with electric mixer on medium speed until well blended.

MIX in all remaining ingredients except pecans; cover. Refrigerate several hours or overnight.

SHAPE into ball; roll in pecans. Serve with assorted **NABISCO** Crackers.

Makes 24 servings, 2 Tbsp. each.

Savory Bruschetta

Prep: 15 min. • Bake: 10 min.

¼ cup olive oil

1 clove garlic, minced

1 loaf (1 lb.) French bread, cut in half lengthwise

1 pkg. (8 oz.) **PHILADELPHIA** Cream Cheese, softened

3 Tbsp. **KRAFT** 100% Grated Parmesan Cheese

2 Tbsp. chopped pitted ripe olives

1 cup chopped plum tomatoes

¼ cup chopped fresh basil

PREHEAT oven to 400°F. Mix oil and garlic; spread onto cut surfaces of bread. Bake 8 to 10 min. or until lightly browned. Cool.

MIX cream cheese and Parmesan cheese with electric mixer on medium speed until blended. Stir in olives.

SPREAD toasted bread halves with cream cheese mixture; top with tomatoes. Cut into 24 slices to serve. Sprinkle with basil.

Makes 2 dozen or 24 servings, 1 slice each.

Baked Crab Rangoon

Prep: 20 min. ● Bake: 20 min.

1 **can (6 oz.) white crabmeat, drained, flaked**

4 **oz. (½ of 8-oz. pkg.) PHILADELPHIA Neufchâtel Cheese, softened**

¼ **cup thinly sliced green onions**

¼ **cup KRAFT Mayo Light Mayonnaise**

12 **wonton wrappers**

PREHEAT oven to 350°F. Mix crabmeat, Neufchâtel cheese, onions and mayo.

SPRAY 12 medium muffin cups with cooking spray. Gently place 1 wonton wrapper in each cup, allowing edges of wrappers to extend above sides of cups. Fill evenly with crabmeat mixture.

BAKE 18 to 20 min. or until edges are golden brown and filling is heated through. Serve warm. Garnish as desired.

Makes 12 servings, 1 wonton each.

Cream Cheese Bacon Crescents

Prep: 15 min. • Bake: 15 min.

1 tub (8 oz.) **PHILADELPHIA** Chive & Onion Light Cream Cheese Spread

3 slices **OSCAR MAYER Bacon, cooked, crumbled**

2 cans (8 oz. each) **reduced fat refrigerated crescent dinner rolls**

PREHEAT oven to 375°F. Mix cream cheese spread and bacon in small bowl until well blended.

SEPARATE each can of dough into 8 triangles each. Cut each triangle in half lengthwise. Spread each dough triangle with 1 generous tsp. cream cheese mixture. Roll up, starting at shortest side of triangle and rolling to opposite point. Place, point sides down, on ungreased baking sheet.

BAKE 12 to 15 min. or until golden brown. Serve warm.

Makes 16 servings, 2 crescents each.

Blue Cheese Mushrooms

Prep: 30 min. • Broil: 3 min.

24 medium fresh mushrooms (1 lb.)

¼ cup sliced green onions

1 Tbsp. butter or margarine

1 pkg. (4 oz.) **ATHENOS** Crumbled Blue Cheese

3 oz. **PHILADELPHIA** Cream Cheese, softened

PREHEAT broiler. Remove stems from mushrooms; chop stems. Cook and stir stems and onions in butter in small skillet on medium heat until tender.

ADD blue cheese and cream cheese; mix well. Spoon evenly into mushroom caps; place on rack of broiler pan.

BROIL 2 to 3 min. or until golden brown. Serve warm.

Makes 2 dozen or 24 servings, 1 mushroom each.

Three Pepper Quesadillas

Prep: 20 min. • Bake: 10 min.

1 cup thin green pepper strips

1 cup thin red pepper strips

1 cup thin yellow pepper strips

½ cup thin onion slices

⅓ cup butter or margarine

½ tsp. ground cumin

1 pkg. (8 oz.) **PHILADELPHIA** Cream Cheese, softened

1 pkg. (8 oz.) **KRAFT** Shredded Sharp Cheddar Cheese

10 **TACO BELL**® **HOME ORIGINALS**® Flour Tortillas

1 jar (16 oz.) **TACO BELL**® **HOME ORIGINALS**® Thick 'N Chunky Salsa

PREHEAT oven to 425°F. Cook and stir peppers and onion in butter in large skillet on medium-high heat until crisp-tender. Stir in cumin. Drain, reserving liquid.

BEAT cream cheese and Cheddar cheese with electric mixer on medium speed until well blended. Spoon 2 Tbsp. cheese mixture onto each tortilla; top each evenly with pepper mixture. Fold tortillas in half; place on ungreased baking sheet. Brush with reserved liquid.

BAKE 10 min. or until heated through. Cut each tortilla into thirds. Serve warm with salsa.

Makes 30 servings, 1 piece each.

TACO BELL® and HOME ORIGINALS® are trademarks owned and licensed by Taco Bell Corp.

Creamy Coconut Dip

Prep: 5 min. plus refrigerating

1 pkg. (8 oz.) **PHILADELPHIA Cream Cheese,** softened

1 can (15 oz.) cream of coconut

1 tub (16 oz.) **COOL WHIP Whipped Topping, thawed**

BEAT cream cheese and cream of coconut in large bowl with wire whisk until well blended.

ADD whipped topping; gently stir until well blended. Cover. Refrigerate several hours or until chilled.

SERVE with **HONEY MAID** Grahams Honey Sticks and cut-up fresh fruit.

Makes 48 servings, 2 Tbsp. each.

Sweet Fruit Dip

Prep: 10 min. plus refrigerating

4 oz. (½ of 8-oz. pkg.) PHILADELPHIA Cream Cheese, softened

1 cup whole berry cranberry sauce

1 cup thawed COOL WHIP Whipped Topping

BEAT cream cheese and cranberry sauce with electric mixer on medium speed until well blended. Gently stir in whipped topping; cover.

REFRIGERATE at least 1 hour or until ready to serve.

SERVE with cut-up fresh fruit dippers.

Makes 16 servings, 2 Tbsp. each.

PHILADELPHIA Cucumber and Herb Dip

Prep: 30 min. plus refrigerating

1 pkg. (8 oz.) PHILADELPHIA Cream Cheese, softened

1 cup finely shredded cucumber, well drained

½ cup **KRAFT** Shredded Swiss Cheese

½ tsp. dill weed

½ tsp. lemon juice

¼ tsp. minced fresh garlic

¼ tsp. salt

MIX all ingredients until well blended; cover.

REFRIGERATE at least 2 hours or until ready to serve.

Makes 18 servings.

SUBSTITUTE: Prepare as directed, using PHILADELPHIA Neufchâtel Cheese.

SPECIAL EXTRA: Serve with assorted NABISCO Crackers and fresh vegetable dippers.

2-Minute Delicious PHILLY Dip

Prep: 5 min.

¼ cup **PHILADELPHIA** Cream Cheese Spread

1 Tbsp. **KRAFT CATALINA** Dressing

2 Tbsp. sliced black olives

  TRISCUIT Thin Crisps

MIX first 3 ingredients until well blended.

SERVE with crackers.

Makes ½ cup dip or 4 servings, 2 Tbsp. dip and 3 crackers each.

VARIATION: Serve with celery sticks instead of/in addition to the crackers.

SUBSTITUTE: Prepare using green olives.

Entrées & Sides

Deep Dish Chicken Pot Pie

Prep: 20 min. ● Bake: 30 min.

1 lb. boneless skinless chicken breasts, cut into 1-inch pieces

¼ cup **KRAFT** Light Zesty Italian Reduced Fat Dressing

4 oz. (½ of 8-oz. pkg.) **PHILADELPHIA** Neufchâtel Cheese, cubed

2 Tbsp. flour

½ cup fat-free reduced-sodium chicken broth

1 pkg. (10 oz.) frozen mixed vegetables, thawed

1 refrigerated pie crust (½ of 15-oz. pkg.)

PREHEAT oven to 375°F. Cook chicken in dressing in large skillet on medium heat 2 min. Add Neufchâtel cheese; cook and stir until melted. Add flour; mix well. Add broth and vegetables; simmer 5 min.

POUR mixture into deep-dish 10-inch pie plate. Arrange pie crust over filling; flute edges. Cut 4 slits in crust to allow steam to escape.

BAKE 30 min. or until crust is golden brown.

Makes 6 servings.

Swordfish with Leek Cream

Prep: 15 min. • Grill: 8 min.

4 swordfish steaks (1 lb.)

2 Tbsp. oil

2 Tbsp. butter or margarine

1 leek, cut into 1-inch strips

4 oz. (½ of 8-oz. pkg.) **PHILADELPHIA** Cream Cheese, cubed

3 Tbsp. dry white wine

½ cup milk

2 Tbsp. chopped fresh parsley

½ tsp. garlic salt

¼ tsp. black pepper

PREHEAT greased grill to high heat.

BRUSH fish with oil. Grill 3 to 4 min. on each side or until fish flakes easily with fork.

MEANWHILE, melt butter in medium skillet on medium heat. Add leeks; cook and stir until tender. Add remaining ingredients; cook on low until cream cheese is melted and mixture is well blended, stirring frequently.

SERVE fish topped with sauce.

Makes 4 servings.

SERVING SUGGESTION: Serve with a hot steamed vegetable and whole grain rolls for an elegant dinner for 4.

SUBSTITUTE: Prepare using PHILADELPHIA Neufchâtel Cheese.

ENTRÉES & SIDES

Stuffed Fiesta Burgers

Prep: 15 min. ● Grill: 18 min.

1 lb. ground beef

1 cup pkg. (1¼ oz.) **TACO BELL® HOME ORIGINALS®** Taco Seasoning Mix

¼ cup **PHILADELPHIA** Chive & Onion Cream Cheese Spread

⅓ cup **KRAFT** Shredded Cheddar Cheese

4 hamburger buns, split, lightly toasted

½ cup **TACO BELL® HOME ORIGINALS®** Thick 'N Chunky Medium Salsa

1 avocado, peeled, pitted and cut into 8 slices

PREHEAT grill to medium heat. Mix meat and seasoning mix. Shape into 8 thin patties. Mix cream cheese spread and shredded Cheddar cheese. Spoon about 2 Tbsp. of the cheese mixture onto center of each of 4 of the patties; top with second patty. Pinch edges of patties together to seal.

GRILL 7 to 9 min. on each side or until cooked through (160°F).

COVER bottom halves of buns with burgers. Top with salsa, avocados and top halves of buns.

Makes 4 servings, 1 burger each.

TACO BELL® and HOME ORIGINALS® are trademarks owned and licensed by Taco Bell Corp.

Spaghetti with Zesty Bolognese

Prep: 10 min. ● Cook: 15 min.

1 small onion, chopped

¼ cup **KRAFT Light Zesty Italian Reduced Fat Dressing**

1 lb. extra lean ground beef

1 can (15 oz.) tomato sauce

1 can (14 oz.) diced tomatoes, undrained

2 Tbsp. **PHILADELPHIA Neufchâtel Cheese**

12 oz. spaghetti, uncooked

¼ cup **KRAFT 100% Grated Parmesan Cheese**

COOK onions in dressing in large skillet on medium heat. Increase heat to medium-high. Add meat; cook, stirring frequently, until browned. Stir in tomato sauce and tomatoes. Bring to boil. Reduce heat to medium-low; simmer 15 min. Remove from heat. Stir in Neufchâtel cheese until well blended.

MEANWHILE, cook pasta as directed on package.

SPOON sauce over pasta. Sprinkle with Parmesan cheese.

Makes 6 servings.

Pasta Primavera Alfredo

Prep: 5 min. • Cook: 15 min.

4 oz. (½ of 8-oz. pkg.) **PHILADELPHIA** Cream Cheese, cubed

¾ cup milk

½ cup **KRAFT** Shredded Parmesan Cheese

¼ cup butter or margarine

¼ tsp. white pepper

¼ tsp. garlic powder

⅛ tsp. ground nutmeg

2 cups small broccoli florets

1 cup chopped carrots

1 pkg. (9 oz.) refrigerated fettuccine

PLACE cream cheese, milk, Parmesan cheese and butter in small saucepan; cook on medium-low heat until cream cheese is completely melted and mixture is well blended, stirring occasionally. Add pepper, garlic powder and nutmeg; stir until well blended.

MEANWHILE, add vegetables and pasta to 2½-qt. boiling water in large saucepan; cook 3 min. Drain.

TOSS pasta mixture with the cream cheese mixture.

Makes 5 servings, 1¼ cups each.

Creamy Roast Beef Sandwiches

Prep: 5 min. • Cook: 15 min.

1 cup sliced onions, separated into rings

1 Tbsp. butter or margarine

6 oz. (¾ of 8-oz. pkg.) **PHILADELPHIA** Cream Cheese, cubed

½ cup milk

1 Tbsp. **KRAFT** Prepared Horseradish

6 pita breads, cut in half

1 lb. shaved deli roast beef

2 medium tomatoes, chopped

2 cups shredded lettuce

COOK and stir onions in butter in medium skillet on medium heat until tender. Add cream cheese and milk; stir. Reduce heat to low; cook until cream cheese is completely melted and mixture is well blended, stirring occasionally. Stir in horseradish.

FILL pita pockets evenly with meat, tomatoes and lettuce.

DRIZZLE with the horseradish sauce.

Makes 6 servings, 2 filled pita halves each.

Italian Five-Cheese Chicken Roll-Ups

Prep: 10 min. • Bake: 35 min.

1 cup **KRAFT** Finely Shredded Italian* Five Cheese Blend, divided

2 oz. (¼ of 8-oz. pkg.) **PHILADELPHIA** Cream Cheese, softened

¼ cup finely chopped green peppers

½ tsp. dried oregano leaves

¼ tsp. garlic salt

4 small boneless skinless chicken breast halves (1 lb.), pounded to ¼-inch thickness

1 cup spaghetti sauce

PREHEAT oven to 400°F. Mix ½ cup of the shredded cheese, the cream cheese, peppers, oregano and garlic salt until well blended. Shape into 4 logs. Place 1 log on one of the short ends of each chicken breast; press into chicken lightly. Roll up each chicken breast tightly, tucking in ends of chicken around filling to completely enclose filling.

PLACE, seam-sides down, in 13×9-inch baking dish sprayed with cooking spray. Spoon spaghetti sauce evenly over chicken; cover with foil.

BAKE 30 min. or until chicken is cooked through (170°F). Remove foil; sprinkle chicken with remaining ½ cup shredded cheese. Bake an additional 3 to 5 min. or until cheese is melted.

Makes 4 servings.

* Made with quality cheeses crafted in the USA.

Family-Favorite Roast Chicken

Prep: 10 min. • Bake: 1 hour 30 min.

1 **(4½-lb.) roasting chicken**

¼ **tsp. black pepper**

⅛ **tsp. salt**

1 **medium lemon, washed**

4 **oz. (½ of 8-oz. pkg.) PHILADELPHIA Cream Cheese, softened**

1 **Tbsp. Italian seasoning**

½ **cup KRAFT Zesty Italian Dressing**

PREHEAT oven to 350°F. Rinse chicken; pat dry with paper towel. Use the tip of a sharp knife to separate the chicken skin from the meat in the chicken breast and tops of the legs. Sprinkle chicken both inside and out with the pepper and salt. Place in 13×9-inch baking dish.

GRATE the lemon; mix the peel with cream cheese and Italian seasoning. Use a small spoon or your fingers to carefully stuff the cream cheese mixture under the chicken skin, pushing the cream cheese mixture carefully toward the legs, being careful to not tear the skin.

CUT the lemon in half; squeeze both halves into small bowl. Add dressing; beat with wire wire whisk until well blended. Drizzle evenly over chicken. Place the squeezed lemon halves inside the chicken cavity. Insert an ovenproof meat thermometer into thickest part of one of the chicken's thighs.

BAKE 1 hour 30 min. or until chicken is no longer pink in center (165°F), basting occasionally with the pan juices.

Makes 8 servings.

Bacon & Tomato Presto Pasta

Prep: 10 min. • Cook: 10 min.

8 slices **OSCAR MAYER** Bacon, chopped

½ cup cherry tomatoes

1 tub (8 oz.) **PHILADELPHIA** Chive & Onion Cream Cheese Spread

1 cup milk

½ cup **KRAFT** 100% Grated Parmesan Cheese

6 cups hot cooked penne pasta

COOK bacon in skillet 5 min. or until bacon is crisp, stirring occasionally. Drain skillet, leaving bacon in skillet. Stir in cherry tomatoes.

ADD cream cheese spread, milk and Parmesan cheese; mix well. Cook until hot and bubbly, stirring frequently.

STIR in pasta.

Makes 8 servings.

Parmesan-Crusted Chicken in Cream Sauce

Prep: 15 min. • Cook: 15 min.

2 cups instant brown rice, uncooked

1 can (14 oz.) fat-free reduced-sodium chicken broth, divided

6 RITZ Crackers, finely crushed

2 Tbsp. KRAFT 100% Grated Parmesan Cheese

4 small boneless skinless chicken breast halves (1 lb.)

⅓ cup PHILADELPHIA Chive & Onion Light Cream Cheese Spread

2 tsp. oil

¾ lb. asparagus spears, trimmed, steamed

COOK rice as directed on package, using 1¼ cups of the broth and ½ cup water.

MEANWHILE, mix cracker crumbs and Parmesan cheese on plate. Rinse chicken with cold water; gently shake off excess water. Dip chicken in crumb mixture, turning each piece over to evenly coat both sides. Place in single layer in lightly greased shallow baking pan. Discard any remaining crumb mixture.

HEAT oil in large nonstick skillet on medium heat. Add chicken; cook 5 to 6 min. on each side or until golden brown on both sides and cooked through (165°F). Place chicken on serving plate; cover to keep warm. Add remaining ½ cup broth and the cream cheese spread to skillet. Cook on medium heat just until mixture comes to boil, stirring constantly. Simmer 3 min. or until sauce is thickened, stirring frequently. Spoon sauce over chicken. Serve with the rice and asparagus.

Makes 4 servings.

Farmhouse Chicken Dinner

Prep: 15 min. • Cook: 30 min.

¼ cup flour

½ tsp. black pepper

4 small bone-in chicken breast halves (1½ lb.), skin removed

¼ cup **KRAFT Light Zesty Italian Reduced Fat Dressing**

2 cups baby carrots

1 onion, cut into wedges

1 can (14½ oz.) fat-free reduced-sodium chicken broth, divided

2 cups instant brown rice, uncooked

4 oz. (½ of 8-oz. pkg.) **PHILADELPHIA Neufchâtel Cheese, cubed**

2 Tbsp. chopped fresh parsley

MIX flour and pepper in shallow dish. Add chicken; turn to evenly coat both sides of each piece with flour mixture. Gently shake off excess flour mixture; set aside. Heat dressing in large nonstick skillet on medium heat. Add chicken, meat-side down; cook 5 to 6 min. or until golden brown. Turn chicken; add carrots, onion and 1 cup of the broth. Cover. Reduce heat to medium-low; simmer 20 min. or until carrots are tender and chicken is cooked through (165°F).

MEANWHILE, cook rice as directed on package. Spoon onto serving platter. Use slotted spoon to remove chicken and vegetables from skillet; place over rice. Cover to keep warm.

ADD Neufchâtel cheese and remaining broth to skillet; increase heat to high. Cook until cheese is melted and sauce is well blended, stirring constantly. Reduce heat to medium-low; simmer 3 to 5 min. or until sauce is slightly thickened, stirring occasionally. Spoon over chicken and vegetables; sprinkle with parsley.

Makes 4 servings.

Creamy Restaurant-Style Tortellini

Prep: 5 min. • Cook: 15 min.

2 pkg. (9 oz. each) refrigerated three-cheese tortellini, uncooked

4 oz. (½ of 8-oz. pkg.) **PHILADELPHIA** Cream Cheese, cubed

1 cup milk

6 Tbsp. **KRAFT 100%** Grated Parmesan Cheese, divided

¼ tsp. black pepper

1 bag (6 oz.) baby spinach leaves

1 cup quartered cherry tomatoes (about ½ pt.)

COOK tortellini as directed on package.

MEANWHILE, place cream cheese in large skillet. Cook on low heat until cream cheese is melted, stirring occasionally. Whisk in milk gradually. Stir in 4 Tbsp. (¼ cup) of the Parmesan cheese and the pepper. Add spinach; stir to coat. Drain pasta. Add to spinach mixture in skillet; mix lightly.

SPRINKLE with tomatoes and remaining 2 Tbsp. Parmesan cheese just before serving.

Makes 6 servings, 1½ cups each.

Easy Cauliflower & Broccoli Au Gratin

Prep: 10 min. • Cook: 13 min.

1 lb. large cauliflower florets

1 lb. large broccoli florets

½ cup water

4 oz. (½ of 8-oz. pkg.) **PHILADELPHIA** Cream Cheese, cubed

¼ cup milk

½ cup **BREAKSTONE'S** or **KNUDSEN** Sour Cream

1½ cups **KRAFT** Shredded Sharp Cheddar Cheese

10 **RITZ** Crackers, crushed

3 Tbsp. **KRAFT** 100% Grated Parmesan Cheese

PLACE cauliflower and broccoli in 2-qt. microwaveable dish. Add water; cover. Microwave on HIGH 8 to 10 min. or until vegetables are tender; drain. Set aside.

MICROWAVE cream cheese and milk in 2-cup microwaveable measuring cup or medium bowl 1 min. or until cream cheese is melted and mixture is well blended when stirred. Add sour cream; mix well. Pour over vegetables; sprinkle with Cheddar cheese. Microwave 2 min. or until cheese is melted.

MIX cracker crumbs and Parmesan cheese. Sprinkle over vegetables.

Makes 10 servings, about ¾ cup each.

White & Gold Pizza

Prep: 20 min. • Bake: 12 min.

- **3** Tbsp. olive oil, divided
- **1** large sweet onion, thinly sliced
- **1** lb. frozen pizza dough, thawed
- **1** large clove garlic, minced
- **4** oz. (½ of 8-oz. pkg.) **PHILADELPHIA** Cream Cheese, softened
- **¾** cup **KRAFT** Shredded Mozzarella Cheese
- **½** cup **DIGIORNO**® Grated Romano Cheese
- **½** tsp. crushed red pepper

PREHEAT oven to 425°F.

HEAT 1 Tbsp. oil in large skillet on medium heat. Add onions; cook 15 to 20 min. or until tender and golden brown, stirring occasionally.

MEANWHILE, place pizza dough on lightly floured baking sheet; pat to 16×12-inch rectangle. Mix garlic and remaining oil; spread onto dough. Bake 10 min.

SPREAD cream cheese onto crust; top with remaining cheeses, onions and crushed pepper. Bake 10 to 12 min. or until crust is golden brown.

Makes 6 servings.

MAKE AHEAD: Caramelized onions can be made ahead of time. Cool, then refrigerate up to 2 days before using as directed.

SMOKED SALMON & CAPERS PIZZA: Prepare as directed, using PHILADELPHIA Salmon Cream Cheese Spread and substituting 2 tsp. capers for the crushed red pepper.

DiGIORNO® is a registered trademark of Nestle, used under license.

232 PHILADELPHIA ENTRÉES & SIDES

Shrimp-in-Love Pasta

Prep: 10 min. ● Cook: 4 min.

¼ lb. linguine, uncooked

1 cup uncooked deveined peeled medium shrimp

2 tomatoes, chopped

½ cup (½ of 8-oz. tub) **PHILADELPHIA** Cream Cheese Spread

1½ cups torn fresh spinach

COOK linguine as directed on package.

MEANWHILE, heat large skillet on medium-high heat. Add shrimp, tomatoes and cream cheese spread; cook and stir 3 to 4 min. or until shrimp are done and mixture is well blended.

DRAIN linguine; place in large bowl. Add spinach; mix lightly. Stir in shrimp mixture.

Makes 2 servings.

SUBSTITUTE: Prepare using **4 oz.** (½ of 8-oz. pkg.) PHILADELPHIA Neufchâtel Cheese.

TO DOUBLE: For **4 servings,** prepare as directed using 1 tub (8 oz.) PHILADELPHIA Cream Cheese Spread and doubling all other ingredients.

Pizza Frittata

Prep: 15 min. ● Broil: 3 min.

6 oz. (¾ of 8-oz. pkg.) **PHILADELPHIA** Cream Cheese, softened

6 eggs

¼ tsp. salt

¼ tsp. each dried basil and oregano

2 Tbsp. butter

1½ cups sliced fresh mushrooms

½ cup chopped green peppers

24 slices **OSCAR MAYER** Pepperoni, coarsely chopped

BEAT cream cheese, eggs, salt and seasonings until well blended.

MELT butter in 10-inch ovenproof skillet on medium heat. Add vegetables; cook and stir 5 min. or until crisp-tender. Stir in pepperoni and cream cheese mixture. Cover; cook 5 min. or until center is almost set.

PREHEAT broiler. Uncover frittata. Broil, 6 inches from heat, 2 to 3 min. or until golden brown.

Makes 6 servings.

SPECIAL EXTRA: Serve topped with pizza sauce.

SERVING SUGGESTION: For added color and texture, serve with a green salad tossed with your favorite KRAFT Light Dressing.

CREATIVE LEFTOVERS: A frittata is a great way to use up leftover vegetables and cheeses in your refrigerator. Cut soft cheese into small cubes or shred hard cheeses before mixing with other filling ingredients in skillet.

Creamy Pasta Primavera

Prep: 15 min. • Cook: 14 min.

3 cups penne pasta, uncooked

2 Tbsp. **KRAFT** Light Zesty Italian Dressing

1½ lb. boneless skinless chicken breasts, cut into 1-inch pieces

2 zucchini, cut into bite-size pieces

1½ cups cut-up fresh asparagus (1-inch lengths)

1 red pepper, chopped

1 cup fat-free reduced-sodium chicken broth

4 oz. (½ of 8-oz. pkg.) **PHILADELPHIA** Neufchâtel Cheese, cubed

¼ cup **KRAFT** Grated Parmesan Cheese

COOK penne in large saucepan as directed on package.

MEANWHILE, heat dressing in large skillet on medium heat. Add chicken and vegetables; cook 10 to 12 min. or until chicken is done, stirring frequently. Add broth and Neufchâtel; cook 1 min. or until Neufchâtel is melted, stirring constantly. Stir in Parmesan.

DRAIN penne; return to pan. Add chicken mixture; toss lightly. Cook 1 min. or until heated through. (Sauce will thicken upon standing.)

Makes 6 servings, 1⅓ cups each.

NUTRITION BONUS: Delight your loved ones with this creamy, yet low-calorie and low-fat, meal that is an easy way to add vegetables to your family's diet.

HOW TO MAKE IT MEATLESS: Omit chicken. Prepare as directed, cooking vegetables until crisp-tender.

Creamy Rice, Chicken & Spinach Dinner

Prep: 10 min. • Cook: 12 min.

¼ cup **KRAFT** Roasted Red Pepper Italian with Parmesan Dressing

1 lb. boneless skinless chicken breasts, cut into strips

1½ cups fat-free reduced-sodium chicken broth

2 cups instant brown rice, uncooked

4 oz. (½ of 8-oz. pkg.) **PHILADELPHIA** Neufchâtel Cheese, cubed

1 pkg. (8 oz.) baby spinach leaves

1 large tomato, chopped

2 Tbsp. **KRAFT** Grated Parmesan Cheese

HEAT dressing in Dutch oven or large deep skillet on medium-high heat. Add chicken; cook 3 min. Stir in broth; bring to a boil. Add rice; stir. Return to a boil; cover. Simmer on medium heat 5 min.

ADD Neufchâtel; cook 2 to 3 min. or until melted, stirring frequently. Add spinach. (Pan will be full.) Cook, covered, 1 min. or until spinach is wilted. Stir gently to mix in spinach.

REMOVE pan from heat. Let stand, covered, 5 min. Stir in tomatoes; top with Parmesan.

Makes 4 servings, 1½ cups each.

SUBSTITUTE: Prepare using KRAFT Light Zesty Italian Dressing.

Tuscan Chicken Simmer

Prep: 5 min. ● Cook: 17 min.

4 small boneless skinless chicken breast halves (1 lb.)

4 oz. (½ of 8-oz. pkg.) **PHILADELPHIA** Cream Cheese, cubed

¼ cup water

¼ cup pesto

2 cups grape or cherry tomatoes

1 cup **KRAFT** Finely Shredded Italian* Five Cheese Blend

HEAT large nonstick skillet sprayed with cooking spray on medium-high heat. Add chicken; cover. Cook 5 to 7 min. on each side or until done (165°F). Remove chicken from skillet; cover to keep warm.

ADD cream cheese, water, pesto and tomatoes to skillet. Cook, uncovered, on medium heat 2 min. or until cream cheese is melted and mixture is well blended, stirring occasionally.

RETURN chicken to skillet. Cook and stir 1 min. or until chicken is coated and heated through. Sprinkle with shredded cheese.

Makes 4 servings.

SERVING SUGGESTION: Spoon over hot cooked spinach fettuccine or ravioli.

HEALTHY LIVING: Save 50 calories and 5 grams of fat per serving by preparing with PHILADELPHIA Neufchâtel Cheese and KRAFT 2% Milk Shredded Mozzarella Cheese.

* Made with quality cheeses crafted in the USA.

New Potatoes in Dill Cream Sauce

Prep: 15 min. • Cook: 50 sec.

2½ lb. new potatoes (about 20), quartered

1 tub (8 oz.) **PHILADELPHIA** Chive & Onion Cream Cheese Spread

¼ cup milk

1 green pepper, chopped

3 Tbsp. chopped fresh dill

COOK potatoes in boiling water in saucepan on medium heat 15 min. or until potatoes are tender; drain.

MEANWHILE, microwave cream cheese spread, milk and peppers in large microwaveable bowl on HIGH 40 to 50 sec. or until cream cheese spread is melted when stirred. Stir in dill until well blended.

ADD potatoes; toss to coat.

Makes 16 servings, about ½ cup each.

SUBSTITUTE: Substitute chopped fresh basil leaves or 2 tsp. dill weed for the chopped fresh dill.

CREATIVE LEFTOVERS: Refrigerate any leftovers. Serve as a cold potato salad, stirring in a small amount of additional milk to thin, if necessary.

Creamy Veggies

Prep: 5 min. • Cook: 13 min.

1 **pkg. (16 oz.) frozen mixed vegetables (California mix)**

¼ **lb. (4 oz.) VELVEETA 2% Milk Pasteurized Prepared Cheese Product, cut into ½-inch cubes**

4 **oz. (½ of 8-oz. pkg.) PHILADELPHIA Fat Free Cream Cheese, cubed**

LAYER ingredients in 1½-qt. microwaveable dish; cover with waxed paper.

MICROWAVE on HIGH 13 min. or until heated through, turning dish after 7 min.

STIR until well blended.

Makes 5 servings.

USE YOUR OVEN: Layer ingredients in 1½-qt. casserole. Bake at 350°F for 55 min. or until heated through. Stir until well blended.

NUTRITION BONUS: This low-fat side dish is a delicious way to eat your vegetables. Not only are the vegetables a good source of both vitamins **A** and **C**, but the cheese also provides calcium.

Garden Vegetable Grill Sandwich

Prep: 10 min. • Grill: 7 min.

- **2** slices red onion (¼-inch thick)
- **2** portobello mushroom caps (4 inch)
- **4** slices zucchini (½-inch thick)
- **¼** cup **KRAFT** Balsamic Vinaigrette Dressing
- **4** whole wheat rolls, split
- **¼** cup **PHILADELPHIA** Garden Vegetable ⅓ Less Fat than Cream Cheese
- **1** tomato, cut into 4 slices
- **4** **KRAFT** 2% Milk Pepperjack Singles

PREHEAT grill to medium heat.

GRILL vegetables 5 to 7 min. or until crisp-tender, turning and brushing occasionally with dressing. Meanwhile, grill rolls, cut-sides down, 1 to 2 min. or until lightly toasted.

REMOVE vegetables and rolls from grill. Cut mushrooms into thin strips. Separate onions into rings.

SPREAD rolls with cream cheese; fill with grilled vegetables, tomatoes and 2% Milk Singles.

Makes 4 servings.

HOW TO GRILL ONIONS: Thread onion slices onto 2 skewers before grilling to prevent the slices from separating into rings when grilling.

Zucchini with Parmesan Sauce

Prep: 10 min. ● Cook: 7 min.

3 zucchini (1 lb.), cut diagonally into ½-inch-thick slices

2 yellow squash, cut diagonally into ½-inch-thick slices

1 red onion, cut into wedges

1 Tbsp. oil

1 tub (8 oz.) **PHILADELPHIA** Chive & Onion Cream Cheese Spread

⅓ cup fat-free milk

¼ cup **KRAFT** Grated Parmesan Cheese

¼ tsp. herb and spice blend seasoning

COOK and stir vegetables in hot oil in large skillet 5 to 7 min. or until crisp-tender.

MEANWHILE, place remaining ingredients in small saucepan; cook on low heat until cream cheese spread is completely melted and mixture is well blended and heated through, stirring occasionally.

SERVE sauce over vegetables.

Makes 8 servings.

HEALTHY LIVING: Save 4 grams of fat per serving by preparing with PHILADELPHIA Chive & Onion ⅓ Less Fat than Cream Cheese.

INDEX

255

METRIC CONVERSION CHART

VOLUME MEASUREMENTS (dry)

1/8 teaspoon = 0.5 mL
1/4 teaspoon = 1 mL
1/2 teaspoon = 2 mL
3/4 teaspoon = 4 mL
1 teaspoon = 5 mL
1 tablespoon = 15 mL
2 tablespoons = 30 mL
1/4 cup = 60 mL
1/3 cup = 75 mL
1/2 cup = 125 mL
2/3 cup = 150 mL
3/4 cup = 175 mL
1 cup = 250 mL
2 cups = 1 pint = 500 mL
3 cups = 750 mL
4 cups = 1 quart = 1 L

VOLUME MEASUREMENTS (fluid)

1 fluid ounce (2 tablespoons) = 30 mL
4 fluid ounces (1/2 cup) = 125 mL
8 fluid ounces (1 cup) = 250 mL
12 fluid ounces (1 1/2 cups) = 375 mL
16 fluid ounces (2 cups) = 500 mL

WEIGHTS (mass)

1/2 ounce = 15 g
1 ounce = 30 g
3 ounces = 90 g
4 ounces = 120 g
8 ounces = 225 g
10 ounces = 285 g
12 ounces = 360 g
16 ounces = 1 pound = 450 g

DIMENSIONS

1/16 inch = 2 mm
1/8 inch = 3 mm
1/4 inch = 6 mm
1/2 inch = 1.5 cm
3/4 inch = 2 cm
1 inch = 2.5 cm

OVEN TEMPERATURES

250°F = 120°C
275°F = 140°C
300°F = 150°C
325°F = 160°C
350°F = 180°C
375°F = 190°C
400°F = 200°C
425°F = 220°C
450°F = 230°C

BAKING PAN SIZES

Utensil	Size in Inches/Quarts	Metric Volume	Size in Centimeters
Baking or Cake Pan (square or rectangular)	8 × 8 × 2	2 L	20 × 20 × 5
	9 × 9 × 2	2.5 L	23 × 23 × 5
	12 × 8 × 2	3 L	30 × 20 × 5
	13 × 9 × 2	3.5 L	33 × 23 × 5
Loaf Pan	8 × 4 × 3	1.5 L	20 × 10 × 7
	9 × 5 × 3	2 L	23 × 13 × 7
Round Layer Cake Pan	8 × 1½	1.2 L	20 × 4
	9 × 1½	1.5 L	23 × 4
Pie Plate	8 × 1¼	750 mL	20 × 3
	9 × 1¼	1 L	23 × 3
Baking Dish or Casserole	1 quart	1 L	—
	1½ quarts	1.5 L	—
	2 quarts	2 L	—